The *Catholic* Topical Memory System

Hiding God's Word In Your Heart and Mind

By Rich Cleveland

Emmaus Journey is an evangelization and discipleship ministry of The Navigators,
an interdenominational religious organization, conducted in and through Catholic parishes.

Adapted by permission from NavPress' *Topical Memory System*

In accord with canon 823 of the Code of Canon Law,
I hereby grant my permission to publish *Hiding God's Word
in Your Heart and Mind* by Richard A. Cleveland.
Most Reverend Michael J. Sheridan
Bishop of Colorado Springs
March 21, 2006

ISBN 0-9785242-0-9
Copyright © 2006 by Emmaus Journey
All rights reserved.

Emmaus Journey
PO Box 63587
Colorado Springs, CO 80962
www.emmausjourney.org

Made and printed in the United States of America

Table of Contents

Why Memorize and Meditate On Sacred Scripture

The reemerging importance of memorization as a valuable aspect of Christian formation is both refreshing and helpful. Pope John Paul II, writing in Catechesis in Our Time, underscores the importance of memorization to the process of catechesis: "In the beginnings of Christian catechesis, which coincided with a civilization that was mainly oral, recourse was had very freely to memorization. Catechesis has since then known a long tradition of learning the principal truths by memorizing."[1]

> *A certain memorization of the words of Jesus, of important Bible passages, of the Ten Commandments, of the formulas of profession of the faith, of the liturgical texts, of the essential prayers, of key doctrinal ideas, etc., ... is a real need, as the Synod Fathers forcefully recalled.*[2]

The Church reminds us of an important principle in overcoming purely mechanical memorization: "The blossoms—if we may call them that—of faith and piety do not grow in the desert places of a memoryless catechesis. What is essential is that texts that are memorized must at the same time be taken in and gradually understood in depth, in order to become a source of Christian life on the personal level and on the community level."[3]

Memorizing key portions of sacred Scripture is important in forming us as Catholics and in acquiring a practical understanding of the Bible. There are many benefits that come from a thorough knowledge of sacred Scripture:

> *Dear brothers, the commands of the Gospel are nothing else than God's lessons, the foundations on which to build up hope,*

the supports for strengthening faith, the food that nourishes the heart. They are the rudder for keeping us on the right course, the protection that keeps our salvation secure. As they instruct the receptive minds of believers on earth, they lead safely to the kingdom of heaven.[4]

We memorize Scripture to:

1. Follow Jesus' example;
2. Enhance our meditation;
3. Equip us for life and ministry; and
4. Learn our way around the Bible.

Follow Jesus' Example. Catholics are first and foremost called to be followers of Jesus Christ. It is him we embrace by faith, his character that we desire the Holy Spirit to reproduce in our lives, and his mission we serve. Jesus practiced certain disciplines from which we, too, can benefit: a life of prayer, participation in a worshipping community, pursuit of the Father's will, and the practice of works of mercy. In addition, Jesus' life and teachings were infused with an intimate and precise knowledge of the Old Testament Scripture. He had it memorized and quoted it frequently to counter the attacks of Satan and to guide people into the knowledge of truth. If Jesus, who is fully God and fully man, valued memorization of Scripture, surely it would be a valuable practice for us as well.

Enhance Our Meditation. Jesus said, "Every one then who hears these words of mine and does them will be like a wise man who built his house upon the rock" (Matthew 7:24). We benefit from sacred Scripture when we are able to think about it, grasp its meaning, and apply it to our lives. Meditation is the key to this process and critically important:

People who have been walking about in a beautiful garden do not like to leave without gathering in their hands four or five flowers to smell and keep for the rest of the day. In the same way, when our soul has carefully considered by meditation a certain mystery, we should select one, two, or three points that we liked the best that are most adapted to our improvement, think frequently about them, and smell them spiritually during the rest of the day.[5]

Scripture memory enables us to prolong meditation on a passage, not only for a day but also for weeks, months, and years. By knowing a passage of Scripture by heart, we are able to meditate on the words of a passage during those times when our hands may be busy, but our minds remain free for meditation, or when it is inconvenient to read the Bible (such as when we are in bed). By recalling a passage we memorized and meditating on it, we are able to prolong its effect.

Equip Us For Life and Ministry. 2 Timothy 3:16, 17 says, "All scripture is inspired by God and profitable for teaching, for reproof, for correction, and for training in righteousness, that the man of God may be complete, equipped for every good work." The following illustration demonstrates how these four characteristics of Scripture prepare and enable us to live a holy life in the midst of our struggles.

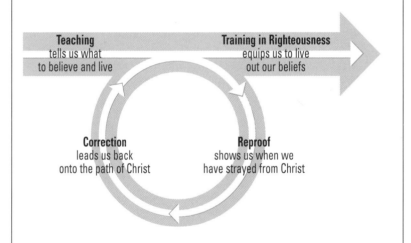

Memorizing key passages of Scripture provides a storehouse of truth from which the Holy Spirit can draw. He will use the truths that you have memorized to "teach you all things, and bring [them] to your remembrance" when they are needed. Those who have practiced the discipline of storing God's words in their heart can testify that at many times, in moments of crisis, or in opportunities for ministry, the Holy Spirit would use some memorized passage to provide the guidance or assistance they needed.

Learn Our Way Around the Bible. Often, when Catholics have an opportunity to share their faith with others, they feel somewhat inept because they do not know their way around the Bible, and do not confidently know many passages or where they can be found in the Bible. This should not be so. Down through the centuries, the Church has been the primary preserver of sacred Scripture, and she is the one to whom the Holy Spirit has clarified and articulated key doctrines like that of the Trinity. As Catholics, we exalt and esteem sacred Scripture in our worship and in our teachings—we of all people should know sacred Scripture and know it well!

As you begin to memorize key verses you will not only gain insight into those passages but they will also provide invisible bookmarks in your memory to help you find your way around the Bible. Jean-Marie Cardinal Lustiger points out, "The word of God must become your mother tongue, must inspire your heart, dwell in your spirit, nourish your life; this familiarity with God which keeps us in his church must become the very heart of your life." [6] As your knowledge of the Bible grows with the help of memorization you will find that this description will become your experience.

We could continue to elaborate on many more values of Scripture memory, but as your heart is attune to the Holy Spirit we are confident that this will be sufficient motivation for you to get started memorizing. Later, after you have memorized some of these passages you will start personally discovering many additional reasons.

Before leaving this section take a moment to record below your primary motivation for wanting to memorize Scripture.

---

[1] *Catechesis in Our Time,* by Pope John Paul II, 55
[2] Ibid.
[3] *General Directory of Catechesis,* The Vatican, 154.15
[4] *Liturgy of the Hours, (LOH),* Vol. II, page 104, from a Treatise by Saint Cyprian
[5] *Introduction to the Devout Life,* by Saint Francis de Sales, page 90
[6] Jean-Marie Cardinal Lustiger, in *Dare to Believe*

Understanding the Process

You can memorize Scripture. The process may seem slow at first as you follow the *Catholic Topical Memory System* and begin building consistent Scripture memory and meditation patterns into your life. But in the long run, *the system saves you time.* Do your best to form good memory habits now as you follow the weekly plans in this book.

Attitude makes the difference. Be confident as you begin memorizing, and you *will* develop the necessary skill.

You can count on God's help as you memorize. Remember his counsel—"These words which I command you this day shall be upon your heart" (Deuteronomy 6:6); and, "Let the word of Christ dwell in you richly" (Colossians 3:16). If this is indeed God's desire we can be confident that he will enable us to do it.

▶ A Look At the System

The *Catholic Topical Memory System* is designed to help you learn four things:

1. How to memorize and meditate on Scripture more effectively.

2. How to apply in your life the verses you memorize.

3. How to review the verses so you can always recall them easily.

4. How to continue memorizing Scripture after you finish this course.

The 70 verses of the Topical Memory System are arranged in five series.

Series A: Live the New Life

Series B: Proclaim Christ

Series C: Rely on God's Resources

Series D: Be Christ's Disciple

Series E: Grow in Christlikeness

Each series has 14 verses and are arranged according to topics. There are two verses for each topic. The recommended pace for learning new verses is two verses per week. Since there are two verses for each topic, you can focus on one topic each week.

Each verse card will look like this:

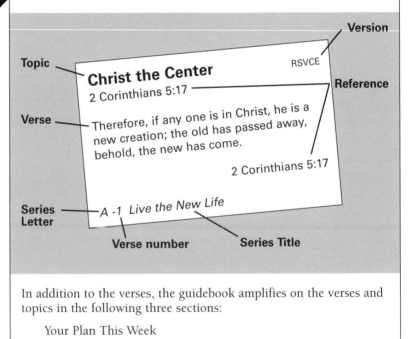

In addition to the verses, the guidebook amplifies on the verses and topics in the following three sections:

Your Plan This Week

Reflection on the Wisdom of the Church

Questions for Meditation

Principles for
Memorizing Scripture

The following principles have proven to be the keys to effective Scripture memory. You'll want to practice and refer to these principles often in the coming weeks:

As you start to memorize a verse—

- Be sure to read and follow the weekly plans given in this book for memorizing the verses. Following this plan will help you gain a deeper understanding of the verses as you learn them.

- Read the suggested Bible passages to provide a context for each verse you memorize.

- Try to gain a clear understanding of what each verse actually means. (You may want to read the verse in other Catholic translations to gain a better understanding of the meaning.)

- Read the verse through several times thoughtfully, aloud or in a whisper. This will help you understand the verse as a whole. Each time you read it, say the topic, reference, verse, and then the reference again.

- Discuss the verse with God in prayer, and continue to seek his help for success in Scripture memory.

While you are memorizing the verse—

- Work on saying the verse aloud as often as possible.
- Learn the topic and reference first.
- After learning the topic and reference, learn the first phrase of the verse. Once you have learned the topic, reference, and first phrase, repeat it several times. Add more phrases after you can quote correctly what you have already learned.
- Think about how the verse applies to you and your daily circumstances.
- Always include the topic and reference as you learn and review the verse.

After you can correctly quote the topic, reference, verse, and reference again—

- Write out the verse. This deepens the verse's impression on your mind.
- Review the verse immediately after learning it, and repeat it frequently in the next few days. This is crucial for firmly fixing the verse in your mind, as we tend to quickly forget things.
- REVIEW! REVIEW! REVIEW! Repetition is the best way to engrave the verses in your memory.

Using This Material in Small-Groups

The *Catholic Topical Memory System* guide book has been designed so that an individual can learn to memorize on their own or so that a group of individuals, such as a men's group or women's fellowship, can learn to memorize together.

Scripture memory can be very beneficial and works, even if it is only done on an individual basis. However, because memorization requires discipline, *it takes a highly motivated individual to complete this course on one's own.*

Consequently, we suggest that you have a like-hearted companion to journey with you as you follow Christ and endeavor to grow in this Christian discipline. As sacred Scripture says, "Two are better than one, because they have a good reward for their toil" (Ecclesiastes 4:9). One of these rewards is mutual accountability that helps you remain faithful to your spiritual goals and increases your chance for success.

So, if you plan on memorizing Scripture as a personal goal, why don't you consider inviting one or two other friends to experience it with you? After all, in a group setting, you will be challenged and encouraged by the spirit, commitment, and progress of the others. In addition, a higher level of *fun* will develop as you take on this challenge together.

The following material provides some helpful suggestions for facilitating discussion and maximizing participation while using it with a small-group:

1. Everyone in the group should have his own copy of *The Catholic Topical Memory System.*

2. During the first week, read and discuss "Why Memorize and Meditate on sacred Scripture" and "Understanding the Process" on pages 5–9. A good way to handle this is to have each individual read these two sections ahead of time and mark in pencil anything that stands out.

3. Have group members look at the "Checklist: *The Catholic Topical Memory System*" (page 16) to get an idea of the topics and verses to be learned. Explain that there are two options open to those participating: each person can either choose to memorize both verses on a topic, as the course was designed to be used, or if an individual has difficulties with memorization, he/she can choose to memorize only one verse per topic.

4. Look ahead to a couple of the weekly assignments so group members can see the information which they will be exposed to each week. Explain that each group session will consist of:

   • 5–10 minutes reviewing the most current memory verses one-on-one with another member of the group. If the week's assignment includes one of the quizzes, review each other's answers to the assignment.

   • 5–10 minutes reading aloud and discussing "Reflection On the Wisdom of the Church." Encourage members to read this material ahead of time and mark ideas they wish to comment on or discuss.

   • 10–20 minutes discussing the week's "Questions for Meditation." As a facilitator, you should think about these questions and passages and develop additional questions.

   • Together, read the topic, reference, verse, and reference for next week's memory verses.

   • Allow individuals to share something from their current faith journeys and conclude with prayer.

Frequently Asked Questions

▶ **Why memorize the topics?**
There are two important reasons for knowing the topics of the verses you memorize: 1) they help you understand the meaning of the verses, and 2) they give you "mental hooks" with which to draw a particular verse from memory when you need it. They also help you recall an appropriate verse when studying the Bible, or when counseling or witnessing to others.

▶ **Why memorize references?**
Knowing the reference for each verse you memorize makes it possible to find the verses in the Bible immediately when you need them for personal use or when helping others. In addition, they earmark important, larger portions of Scripture which you can refer to when needed.

The best way to remember the reference is to say it before and after the verse. This will connect the reference and the verse in your mind.

When learning or reviewing a verse, make it a habit to say the topic first, then the reference, then the verse, and then the reference again at the end. This may seem tedious at first, but it is important —and it works!

▶ **When is the best time to memorize?**
Memorizing verses is easiest when you can concentrate without distraction. Two of the best times are just before you go to bed at night and just before or after your morning devotional time. A few minutes at lunchtime or just before supper may also work well for you. In addition use spare moments during the day—such as while you walk, wait in line at the grocery store, or are otherwise idle—to review your verses. Develop the habit of carrying your verse pack with you.

▶ **Why learn each verse by heart?**
Have as your aim to always quote a verse word-perfectly since it is easier to learn verses correctly at first. Knowing and reciting verses by heart will give you greater confidence when using them, as well as make it easier to review them later.

The Catholic Topical Memory System

Each week, place a check next to the reference of the verses you have successfully memorized.

Series A: Live the New Life

Christ the Center	☐ 2 Corinthians 5:17	☐ Galatians 2:20
Sacramental Life	☐ 1 Peter 2:5	☐ Acts 2:41a–42
Obedience to Christ	☐ Romans 12:2	☐ John 14:21
The Word	☐ 2 Timothy 3:16	☐ Joshua 1:8
Prayer	☐ Matthew 6:6	☐ Philippians 4:6–7
Community	☐ Matthew 18:20	☐ Hebrews 10:24–25
Evangelization	☐ Matthew 4:19	☐ Romans 1:16

Series B: Proclaim Christ

All Have Sinned	☐ Romans 5:12	☐ Isaiah 53:6
Sin's Penalty	☐ Romans 6:23	☐ Hebrews 9:27
Christ Paid the Penalty	☐ Romans 5:8	☐ 1 Peter 3:18
Unmerited Salvation	☐ Ephesians 2:8–9	☐ Titus 3:5
Personal Response	☐ John 1:12	☐ Romans 10:9–10
Assurance of God's Mercy	☐ Philippians 1:6	☐ 1 John 5:13
Be Baptized	☐ Acts 2:38	☐ Galatians 3:26–27

Series C: Rely on God's Resources

His Spirit	☐ John 14:26	☐ 1 Corinthians 2:12
His Presence	☐ Corinthians 10:16	☐ John 6:55–56
His Strength	☐ Isaiah 41:10	☐ Philippians 4:13
His Faithfulness	☐ Lamentations 3:22–23	☐ Numbers 23:19
His Peace	☐ Isaiah 26:3	☐ 1 Peter 5:7
His Provision	☐ Ephesians 6:10–11	☐ Philippians 4:19
His Help in Temptation	☐ Hebrews 2:18	☐ 1 Corinthians 10:13

Series D: Be Christ's Disciple

Put Christ First	☐ Matthew 6:33	☐ Luke 9:23
Pursue Holiness	☐ 1 John 2:15–16	☐ Romans 12:1
Confess Sins?	☐ Psalm 32:5	☐ 1 John 1:9
Be Steadfast	☐ 1 Corinthians 15:58	☐ Hebrews 12:3
Serve Others	☐ Mark 10:45	☐ Galatians 6:10
Give Generously	☐ Proverbs 3:9–10	☐ 2 Corinthians 9:6–7
Develop World Vision	☐ Acts 1:8	☐ Matthew 28:19–20

Series E: Grow in Christlikeness

Love	☐ John 13:34–34	☐ 1 John 3:18
Humility	☐ Philippians 2:3–4	☐ 1 Peter 5:5–6
Purity	☐ Ephesians 5:3–4	☐ 1 Peter 2:11
Honesty	☐ Ephesians 4:25	☐ Acts 24:16
Faith	☐ Hebrews 11:6	☐ Romans 4:20–21
Good Works	☐ Ephesians 2:10	☐ Matthew 5:16
Do God's Will	☐ Ephesians 5:17	☐ 1 Peter 4:1–2

Live the New Life

Dawson Trotman, founder of The Navigators, developed a simple illustration called
the "Wheel Illustration" to demonstrate
what he considered to be the essentials of
living a well-balanced, Christ-centered life.

THE OBEDIENT CHRISTIAN — Prayer — Witnessing — CHRIST — Fellowship — The Word — IN ACTION

Christ, represented by the hub in this illustration, is the motivating source and the power
we need to live a life pleasing to him. As Catholics,
we would agree that Christ is the center of our life and
existence, but in addition, we also understand and believe that the
Holy Spirit, through the sacramental life, draws us ever more deeply
into the life of Christ through his Body the Church. The Sacraments
are various manifestations of Jesus' presence in the Church and
enable us to open ourselves to Christ's grace more fully. "*He* is the
baptized one and the confirmed one; he is the really present one; he
is the reconciler; *he* is the priest; *he* is the lover; *he* is the healer.
Thus, it is not as if Jesus Christ is another sacrament *alongside* the
seven sacraments. *He* is *the* sacrament; …"[1] The second inner ring
represents this Sacramental Life which, like the spokes of a wheel,
provides the basic means whereby Christ's power reaches
our lives and flows through our life to others

The rim of the wheel represents you, the
Obedient Christian, responding to Christ's
reign in your life through wholehearted obedience to his revealed will. This obedience
to Christ will be manifest by our thoughts,
words, and deeds expressed both toward
fellow believers and toward unbelievers
whom we encounter in our world.

The vertical spokes represent two

OBEDIENCE — Prayer — SACRAMENTAL LIFE — Evangelization — CHRIST — Community — The Word — TO CHRIST

means by which we are able to develop our relationship with Christ, The Word, and prayer. In various contexts, the expression, "The Word" represents different meanings: Jesus the *Logos* of God; the Bible as the written word of God; or revealed truth (i.e., "a single sacred deposit of the Word of God"2) that includes both sacred Scripture and sacred tradition. "The Word" and prayer are critically important in the sacramental and liturgical life of a community and in the personal spiritual life of the individual. **It is through "The Word" that the Father communicates to us, and it is through prayer that we are able to communicate to the Father.**

The horizontal spokes represent our relationship with believers and non-believers. We should be part of a parish community where we can be ministered to and where we serve others. As we live in community, we become formed as Christ's followers and are equipped to serve him.

One of the ways that we are mandated to serve him is through a life of evangelization. Evangelization, as we will learn in the subsequent weeks, is our primary task and a mandate from Christ which we are to fulfill as we go forth into the world to bring about conversion to all and in all spheres of society.

Like a wheel, our life runs most smoothly when the various aspects of the Christian life are present and in balance. When one aspect is missing or unbalanced, our lives often become unstable and ineffective.

The verses in **Series A: Live the New Life** will help you discover the importance of these foundational principles for keeping Christ in the center of your life:

Christ the Center—2 Corinthians 5:17 and Galatians 2:20
Sacramental Life—1 Peter 2:5 and Acts 2:41a–42
Obedience to Christ—Romans 12:2 and John 14:21
The Word—2 Timothy 3:16 and Joshua 1:8
Prayer—Matthew 6:6 and Philippians 4:6–7
Community—Matthew 18:20 and Hebrews 10:24–25
Evangelization—Matthew 4:19 and Romans 1:16

Notes

---

[1] *Catholicism,* by Richard P. McBrien, page 789
[2] *The Dogmatic Constitution on Divine Revelation,* Vatican II, 10

Topic: Christ the Center

Verses: 2 Corinthians 5:17 and Galatians 2:20

Your Plan This Week

1. Before beginning to memorize these first two verses, read through the "Principles for Memorizing Scripture" on page 10. Check here when you have completed reading this. _____

2. Put your name, address, and telephone number on the small identification card. Place this card and the 14 Series A verse cards in your verse pack.

3. Use the first two days of the week to memorize 2 Corinthians 5:17, and the third and fourth days to learn Galatians 2:20.

4. Use the remainder of the week to review and meditate on both verses, making sure you know them well. It is especially helpful to understand the verses' context. The "Questions for Meditation" will help you understand these verses.

5. At the end of the week, review by writing out your verses from memory or by quoting them to someone else. Then check off these two verses on the checklist on page 16. (Use this same procedure each week.)

Reflection on the Wisdom of the Church

It can be demanding to relate to people as salt and light, and to continually give ourselves to others through good deeds. The Christian who attempts to do so by his own strength and without the right motives usually ends up either self-righteous and proud, or discouraged and burned out. It is crucial that Christ's life and love become the power source at the center of our lives.

Saint John Eudes adequately captures the essence and absolute necessity of Christians having Christ as the center and power source of their life:

> You belong to the Son of God, but more than that, you ought to be in him as the members are in the head. All that is in you must be incorporated into him. You must receive life from him and be ruled by him. There will be no true life for you except in him, for he is the one source of true life. Apart from him you will find only death and destruction. Let him be the only source of your movements, of the actions and strengths of your life. He must be both the source and the purpose of your life, ...[1]

This is a profound statement of what this week's second memory verse means when it says, "I have been crucified with Christ; it is no longer I who live, but Christ who lives in me; and the life I now live in the flesh I live by faith in the Son of God, who loved me and gave himself for me" (Gal 2:20).

We are happiest only when we allow Jesus to become for us what he was for Saint John Eudes, the center of our existence, where we "have one breath with him, one soul, one life, one will, one mind, one heart. And he must be your breath, heart, love, life, your all."[2]

Questions for Meditation

2 Corinthians 5:17 (For context, read 2 Corinthians 5:14–21)

- What is the time frame for becoming a new creature in Christ? Is it immediate, a process, or both? Explain.

- What is the motivation for living the new life as seen in vs. 14–21?

- What "old" area is Christ removing from your life?

- What aspects of newness has Christ brought to your life?

Galatians 2:20 (for context, read Galatians 2:17–21)

- What affect should being crucified with Christ have on your thoughts, emotions, or behavior?

- How does knowledge of Christ's love for you help you to live a life of faith for him?

Notes

---

[1] A treatise on the admirable heart of Jesus, by Saint John Eudes, LOH Vol. IV, page 1331
[2] Ibid, 1332

Topic: Sacramental Life

Verses: 1 Peter 2:5 and Acts 2:41a–42

▶ **Your Plan This Week**

1. Read "How to Review Memory Verses with Someone Else" on page 23. Check here when you have read it. _____

2. Follow the same pattern for learning new verses as you did last week—use the first two days of the week to learn 1 Peter 2:5, and the next two days to learn Acts 2:41a–42. Review all four of the verses you have memorized during the rest of the week to deepen your understanding of them.

3. Carry your verse pack with you and use spare moments during the day for review and meditation.

4. At the end of the week, check your understanding of these verses as you did before by writing out your new verses from memory or quoting them to someone else.

5. REVIEW: Each day this week, review the first two verses in Series A —2 Corinthians 5:17 and Galatians 2:20.

▶ **Reflection on the Wisdom of the Church**

The Sacraments and the sacramental life have the unique ability to introduce us to the mystery of salvation by enabling us to experience Christ's saving presence in our life in a unique way. The Sacraments were given to the Church to assist us in our worship of God and to enable us to actively receive more fully his grace into our lives.

> " 'Seated at the right hand of the Father' and pouring out the Holy Spirit on his Body which is the Church, Christ now acts through the sacraments he instituted to communicate his grace."[1]

Sacraments are outward signs of our faith, our unity, and Jesus' presence. Though many aspects of salvation can be experienced on an individual basis, the Sacraments are not individual acts of devotion, but rather are acts of the Church that we as individuals can only participate in within community.

"Sacraments are 'powers that come forth' from the Body of Christ, which is ever-living and life-giving. They are actions of the Holy Spirit at work in his Body, the Church. They are 'the master-works of God' in the new and everlasting covenant."[2] Though the

Sacraments are the action and work of the Holy Spirit, the Church teaches two balancing truths, the first being that "It is not the personal merit of the recipient that causes grace to be received." Yet, at the same time it recognizes the need for recipients of the Sacraments to have, in the words of St. Thomas Aquinas a "right disposition" of faith in and devotion to God. Let us avail ourselves of this means of grace and strength!

Questions for Meditation

1 Peter 2:5 (For context, read 1 Peter 2:4–12)

- Identify the various terms used to describe Christ's followers. Which one is most significant to you?

- What are the roles and responsibilities of his people in this passage?

- Where do you see evidence of the sacramental life in this passage?

Acts 2:41a–42 (For context, read Acts 2:37–47)

- What elements of the sacramental life do you see in this passage?

- What do you think caused the evangelization results in verse 47?

- What evidence can you see in this passage of "right disposition" in the lives of these new Christians?

Notes

---

[1] *Catechism of the Catholic Church*, 1084
[2] Ibid, 1116

How to Review Memory Verses
With Someone Else

Memorizing and reviewing Scripture with one or more friends will provide mutual encouragement, as well as opportunities to discuss difficulties in memorization. You will also be helped by having someone with whom to share how God is using the verses in your life. Endeavor to review with another person at least once or twice a week.

▶ **Follow this Procedure:**

1. One person holds the other person's verse cards, and calls out the topic and reference on the first card. The other person then repeats the topic and reference, and goes on to quote the entire verse and the reference again at the end. Then go on to other cards in the same way.

2. First review the memory verses you know best.

3. Speak your verses clearly and not too rapidly so you can be easily understood.

4. While the other person is quoting his/her verses, be helpful and encouraging. Do all you can to assure the other's success.

5. When the other person makes a mistake, signal this by shaking your head or simply saying no. Give the person verbal help only if they asks you.

6. Once the other person has realized his mistake, have him/her repeat the entire verse word-perfectly before going on.

7. Make it your goal to repeat each verse verbatim.

▶ Remember that Scripture memory is not an end in itself. It must be followed by prayerful meditation, obedience, and application.

- *Scripture memory* puts sacred Scripture on your *mind.*
- *Prayerful meditation* puts sacred Scripture in your *heart.*
- *Obedience* puts sacred Scripture into *action.*

Topic: Obedience to Christ

Verses: Romans 12:2 and John 14:21

Your Plan This Week

1. Follow the same pattern for learning new verses as you did last week—use the first two days of the week to learn Romans 12:2, and the next two days to learn John 14:21.

2. Carry your verse pack with you and use spare moments during the day for review and meditation.

3. At the end of the week, review as you did before by writing out your new verses from memory or quoting them to someone else.

4. REVIEW: Each day this week, review the first four verses in Series A.

Reflection on the Wisdom of the Church

Obedience is often viewed by us in the same way as the term "submission." In our American culture, we have elevated personal freedom as the one right which we dare not relinquish. Consequently, we often see any authority as an infringement upon our freedom, and resist submitting in obedience to anyone or anything unless the consequence of not doing so compels us. Unfortunately, this insistence on personal freedom often negatively affects our Christian life by deceiving us into thinking that obedience to God is optional and that we can pick and choose which of God's desires we will obey.

As long as we see obedience as requiring us to submit to something or someone unpleasant, we will struggle with living our new life in Christ. Rather than being compelled to do something, the biblical understanding of obedience is the natural outworking of faith in God's will and an expression of our love and desire to please him. Obedience simply gives us an opportunity to express our faith, love and devotion to God in a tangible way.

Love motivates us to obey and converts obedience from a grudging duty into an act of devotion. In this week's second memory verse, Jesus promises to make himself known more fully to the person who lovingly obeys him. This is love responding to love. In addition, the Holy Spirit helps us discover Christ's will and the areas in which he wants us to obey him as we pray for guidance, reflect on Scripture, and listen to the Church's teaching. "His commandments are not simply moral precepts: they involve a whole way of life in loving union with him."[1] It is this same orientation which Jesus manifested when he said that his "food" or purpose was to do the Father's will. Obedience is not simply adherence to a set of rules, rather, it is a heart and will responsive to seek out and do all that pleases the Father.

Questions for Meditation

Romans 12:2 (For context, read Romans 11:33 —12:2)

- How does conformity to the world express itself?
- Why do our minds have to be transformed before we can recognize and do God's will?
- How does Scripture memory help to transform our minds?

John 14:21 (For context, read John 14:15–21)

- What is the proof of our love to God?
- According to this verse, what responsibilities do you have?
- What is the difference between *having* his commandments and *keeping* them?
- What is the promise(s) of John 14:21?
- What is the relationship between obedience and doing God's will?

Notes

---

[1] *The Gospel According to John*, (The Anchor Bible Vol. 29A) by Raymond Brown, page 638.

Topic: The Word

Verses: 2 Timothy 3:16 and Joshua 1:8

Your Plan This Week

1. Follow the same pattern—spend the first two days of the week learning 2 Timothy 3:16 and the next two days learning Joshua 1:8. Use the rest of the week for review. Remember to review.

2. Remember that it is helpful to write out the verse while you are trying to deepen its impression on your mind.

3. REVIEW: Each day this week, review the six verses you have already learned.

Reflection on the Wisdom of the Church

The Bible is foundational to our life and health in Jesus Christ. The Psalmist says that the Scripture revives the soul, makes wise the simple, causes joy in our heart and enlightens our understanding (Psalms 19:7–10). The individual who is serious about following God will become a student of sacred Scripture, finding that as he meditates on it and aligns his life with it that the benefits will far outweigh the effort expended.

We do not primarily read sacred Scripture to increase our intellect but because "the Father who is in heaven comes lovingly to meet his children, and talks with them,"[1] through the pages of Scripture. As we commune with the Father through the Scripture we find "strength for their [our] faith, food for the soul, and a pure and lasting fount of spiritual life."[2]

Reading Scripture is not a duty, it is a necessity of life. The Church has always greatly valued sacred Scripture as foundational to our well being and happiness both in this life and in the life to come as the following quote illustrates:

"If you encounter grief, dive into them [sacred Scripture] as into a chest of medicines; take from them comfort for your trouble, whether it be loss, or death, or bereavement over the loss of relations. Don't simply dive into them. Swim in them. Keep them constantly in your mind. The cause of all evils is the failure to know the Scriptures well." [3]

Sacred Scripture is in fact our source of all these things and many more. The person who is wise will develop the life-long habit of hearing, reading, studying, meditating and praying the Scripture. In so doing, as the Psalmist point out, he will become "like a tree planted by streams of water, that yields its fruit in its season, and its leaf does not wither. In all that he does, he prospers."

Questions for Meditation

2 Timothy 3:16 (For context, read 2 Timothy 3:14–17)

- Refer to the illustration on page 7 to get a visual picture of this verse.

- How should knowing that God inspired sacred Scripture affect you?

- What significance do you see in the listing order of the four benefits of Scripture?

Joshua 1:8 (For context, read Joshua 1:6–9)

- What is the value of meditating on Scripture?

- What kind of prosperity and success do you think this verse refers to?

Notes

---

[1] *The Dogmatic Constitution on Divine Revelation* (VI, 21), Vatican II.
[2] Ibid.
[3] John Chrysostom, "Homilies on Colossians" as cited in *Reading Scripture with the Church Fathers*, page 96

Topic: Prayer

Verses: Matthew 6:6 and Philippians 4:6–7

Your Plan This Week

1. As you learn and meditate on these new verses, plan to set aside a special time of prayer this week, with these verses fresh in your mind.

2. REVIEW: At least once each day this week, review all of the eight verses you have learned in Series A.

Reflection on the Wisdom of the Church

"Nothing is equal to prayer; for what is impossible it makes possible, what is difficult, easy, ... For it is impossible, utterly impossible, for the man who prays eagerly and invokes God ceaselessly ever to sin."[1] The Catechism, recognizing the essential difference that prayer makes in our life says that "prayer is a vital necessity."[2]

One would certainly come to that conclusion upon observing the life of Jesus. In the Gospels, we see him frequently praying, rising early to pray, finding solitude to pray, teaching his disciples to pray, and prior to his Passion, finding solace in prayer. We will never experience true holiness if we do not learn to pray.

> *Since prayer places our intellect in the brilliance of God's light and exposes our will to the warmth of his heavenly love, nothing else so effectively purifies our intellect of ignorance and our will of depraved affections.*[3]

We learn to pray by praying. Of course, there are valuable books that can help us understand the various kinds of prayer and give us perspective on prayer, but in the end, we learn to pray by praying. Early in their encounter with Jesus, his disciples recognized that he had a unique prayer relationship with the Father; consequently, they asked Jesus, "Lord, teach us to pray." Like the disciples, we need to recognize how important it is to have a competent prayer life and ask the Lord to also teach us to pray.

Questions for Meditation

Matthew 6:6 (For context, read Matthew 6:1–8)

- What principle do you think Jesus was teaching when he said, "go into your room and shut the door and pray?"

- What other principles of prayer do you find in this passage?

Philippians 4:6–7 (For context, read Philippians 4:4–9)

- In what situations are we to pray?

- What is the difference between prayer, supplication, and thanksgiving?

- What should be your response if your heart is not at peace?

Notes

[1] St. John Chrysostom, *De Anna*, CCC 2744.
[2] *Catechism of the Catholic Church*, 2744.
[3] St. Francis de Sales, *Introduction to the Devout Life*, The Necessity of Prayer.

Topic: Community
Verses: Matthew 18:20 and Hebrews 10:24–25

▶ **Your Plan This Week**

1. It takes time and faithful effort to establish a good habit that will last a lifetime. Each week, conscientiously follow the pattern you have learned in earlier weeks for memorizing new verses.

2. Remember to use your Bible to give you the context of each verse you memorize.

3. As you learn these verses on community, evaluate the amount of time you spend with other Christians, as well as the quality of that time. Does it meet biblical standards?

4. DAILY REVIEW: Each day, review the first 10 verses in Series A.

▶ **Reflection on the Wisdom of the Church**

God never intended the Christian life to be lived in isolation, but rather to be lived in community with one another. Christ himself "chose to be born and grow in the bosom of the holy family of Joseph and Mary. The Church is nothing other than 'the family of God.'"[1]

The concept of community is derived from the *Doctrine of the Communion of Saints,* which speaks of the *one* Body of Christ made up of all believers. "The term 'communion of saints' therefore has two closely linked meanings: communion 'in holy things *(sancta)'* and 'among holy persons *(sancti).'*"[2] As we participate in this greater communion of saints, the Holy Spirit also leads us to participate at a local level through a local parish or among smaller units of people with similar interests and calling.

We can all find things that are wrong with "church" but the reality is that Christ loves the Church, it was his idea (Matt. 16:18); Christ obtained the Church with his blood (Acts 20:28); he is its head (Eph. 1:22); its first and preeminent member (Col. 1:18); it is his Body (Col. 1:24); and to it God appointed and established leadership for building up his Body (1 Cor. 12:28) and for demonstrating his power and presence to the world (Eph. 3:10). No Christian who is serious about following Christ can afford to separate himself/herself from dwelling in communion and community with the Church.

Living in a healthy community relationship with others in the Body of Christ is essential to our growth, our perseverance, and our service. It isn't always easy, as Fr. Henri J. Nouwen points out: "Nothing is sweet or easy about community. Community is a fellowship of people who do not hide their joys and sorrows but make them visible to each other in a gesture of hope."[3]—But community is always necessary.

Questions for Meditation

Matthew 18:20 (For context, read Matthew 18:15–20)

- What do you think it means to come together in Jesus' name?

- What affect to you think it would have if we could become consciously aware of Jesus' presence when we are with other Christians?

Hebrews 10:24–25 (For context, read Hebrews 10:19–25)

- How do others encourage you to love and do good deeds?

- What do you think causes people to not go to church or to not participate in community with other Christians?

Notes

[1] *Catechism of the Catholic Church* 1655
[2] Ibid, 948
[3] Fr. Henri J. Nouwen, in *Can You Drink This Cup*

Topic: Evangelization
Verses: Matthew 4:19 and Romans 1:16

Your Plan This Week

1. Who are the people in your life with whom you would like to share your faith in Christ? You may want to make a list of these persons, and use the list to pray for them and to plan for opportunities to talk with them about their spiritual journey.

2. DAILY REVIEW: Each day, review the first 14 verses in Series A. *Your minimum goal should be to repeat each verse once a day.* However, the more time you spend on your verses, the more you will benefit.

Reflection on the Wisdom of the Church
Sharing our faith with another need not be a difficult and mysterious thing. Evangelization can simply be a friend telling a friend about a friend. It is a mandate given to the Church and consequently, as members of the Church, it is given to us as well. Pope Paul VI and Pope John Paul II wrote encyclicals not only declaring that it is our responsibility to witness to the Gospel, but also that it is the world's right to hear it.

Pope Paul VI did much to bring the issue of evangelization to the forefront of our thinking, as the following quotation attests.

> *The Good News proclaimed by the witness of life sooner or later has to be proclaimed by the word of life. There is no true evangelization if the name, the teachings, the life, the promises, the kingdom and the mystery of Jesus of Nazareth, the Son of God are not proclaimed.*[1]

Evangelization involves a two-fold process. Christians, by living a righteous life, are used by the Holy Spirit to attract and draw people to Christ and cause them to wonder and ask what makes these followers of Jesus different. This is what Pope Paul calls "the witness of an authentically Christian life."[2]

Christians then have the responsibility to verbally share Jesus and the Good News with these inquirers. This, the Church teaches, is both the laity's privilege and responsibility

In the "Proclaim Christ" series you will learn several helpful verses for sharing the Good News. In the meantime, simply tell your personal story of faith.

Questions for Meditation

Matthew 4:19 (For context, read Matthew 4:18–22)

- What part of this verse is a command, and what part is a promise?
- Who were these words spoken to and how did they respond?
- How are fishing and evangelization similar or different?

Romans 1:16 (For context, read Romans 1:11–17)

- How does this verse show that the Gospel is for all people?
- What would make someone ashamed, or perhaps embarrassed, to talk with another about Jesus and the Good News?
- How would you define the power of the Gospel?

Notes

---

[1] *On Evangelization In The Modern World* by Pope Paul VI, paragraph 22
[2] Ibid, paragraph 41

Proclaim Christ

Pope John Paul II spoke of the need to proclaim "the living and personal Gospel, Jesus Christ himself" and said "The lay faithful have an essential and irreplaceable role in this announcement and in this testimony."[1] It is important to know that sharing our faith need not be a difficult or scary proposition but rather a simple recounting of our own faith journey, or a conversation with others over a simple Gospel illustration.

In the 1300's, God gave St. Catherine of Siena the image of a bridge to illustrate aspects of salvation in Christ. In deep mystical, contemplative prayer the Father communicated to St. Catherine the life of promise he planned for us

I had created them in my image and likeness so that they might have eternal life, sharing in my being and enjoying my supreme eternal tenderness and goodness.[2]

But he also communicated to Saint Catherine that we have a problem. "Because of their sin they never reached this goal and never fulfilled my truth, for sin closed heaven and the door of mercy."[3] Thus the Father graciously explained that he had made a way out of this dilemma by the provision of Jesus Christ.

I will make of my Son a bridge ... a bridge of the Word, my only-begotten Son."[4]

St. Catherine's analogy of Jesus being a bridge from earth to the Father very effectively communicates that man has a dilemma caused by sin separating us from God; that eternal life is a hope that is attainable; and that Jesus is the means of salvation. This Gospel message we are to proclaim can be encapsulated in a simple but powerful diagram—a bridge illustration. The next 14 verses you will be memorizing will enable you talk through the various aspects of the Gospel. In addition, the questions which you will be thinking about each week are excellent questions which you can use to discuss and explain the Gospel as you interact with others. **It is important when using Scripture to explain the Good News that you graciously raise questions in a manner that will enable the person to comprehend the truth.**

The verses in **Series B: Proclaim Christ** will help you communicate the basic message of salvation to those who have yet to make a decision to become a follower of Christ:

All Have Sinned—Romans 5:12 and Isaiah 53:6
Sin's Penalty—Romans 6:23 and Hebrews 9:27
Christ Paid the Penalty—Romans 5:8 and 1 Peter 3:18
Unmerited Salvation—Ephesians 2:8–9 and Titus 3:5
Personal Response—John 1:12 and Romans 10:9–10
Assurance of God's Mercy—Philippians 1:6 and 1 John 5:13
Be Baptized—Acts 2:38 and Galatians 3:26–27

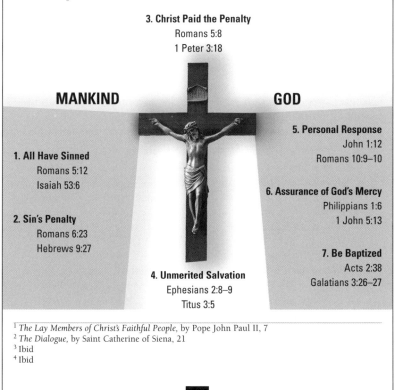

3. Christ Paid the Penalty
Romans 5:8
1 Peter 3:18

MANKIND

GOD

5. Personal Response
John 1:12
Romans 10:9–10

1. All Have Sinned
Romans 5:12
Isaiah 53:6

6. Assurance of God's Mercy
Philippians 1:6
1 John 5:13

2. Sin's Penalty
Romans 6:23
Hebrews 9:27

7. Be Baptized
Acts 2:38
Galatians 3:26–27

4. Unmerited Salvation
Ephesians 2:8–9
Titus 3:5

---

[1] *The Lay Members of Christ's Faithful People,* by Pope John Paul II, 7
[2] *The Dialogue,* by Saint Catherine of Siena, 21
[3] Ibid
[4] Ibid

Topic: All Have Sinned

Verses: Romans 5:12 and Isaiah 53:6

▶ **Your Plan This Week**

1. Review again the "Principles for Memorizing Scripture" on page 11 to see if there are any principles you are overlooking. Place a check here when you have reviewed these principles.
   _____

2. Follow the same pattern in learning the Series B verses as you did in memorizing Series A. At the end of the week, remember to review your progress by writing out your new verses from memory or quoting them to someone else.

3. DAILY REVIEW: All 14 verses of Series A. (You can keep the Series A cards in one side of your verse pack and Series B in the other.)

▶ **Reflection on the Wisdom of the Church**

Humankind has, since the beginning of the world, been harnessed with the problem of sin and the evil that it works in our lives and in the world. Along with sin's harsh societal consequences comes a nagging guilt and subsequent dread of the consequences of our wrongful behavior. By attempting to assuage our guilt, we compensate for the awareness of sin in many ways, from self-denial to self-inflicted punishment. What is needed is a proper understanding of our sinfulness.

It is this proper understanding of our sin which enables our hearts and minds to be receptive to the message of redemption.

> Man, tempted by the devil, let his trust in his Creator die in his heart and abusing his freedom, disobeyed God's command. This is what man's first sin consisted of. All subsequent sin would be disobedience toward and lack of trust in his goodness.[1]

> Without the knowledge Revelation gives of God we cannot recognize sin clearly and are tempted to explain it as merely a developmental flaw, a psychological weakness, a mistake, or the necessary consequence of an inadequate social structure, etc. Only in the knowledge of God's plan for man can we grasp that sin is an abuse of the freedom that God gives to created persons so that they are capable of loving him and loving another.[2]

"What Revelation makes known to us is confirmed by our own experience. For when man looks into his own heart he finds that he is drawn towards what is wrong and sunk in many evils which cannot come from his good creator."[3]

Questions for Meditation

Romans 5:12 (For context, read Romans 5:8–14)

- What is God's response to our sinful nature?
- How would you define sin?
- According to this verse, what are the two sources of sin?
- What are the consequences of sin?

Isaiah 53:6 (For context, read Isaiah 53:4–9)

- How is sin described in this passage?
- How does this verse show that Christ's crucifixion was part of God's plan?
- List the action phrases used to describe Jesus' Passion. Write a brief prayer of thanksgiving for what he endured for you.

Notes

[1] *Catechism of the Catholic Church* 397
[2] *Ibid,*387
[3] *Pastoral Constitution On The Church In The Modern World,* 13

How to Meditate on the Scriptures

Scripture meditation is not mind-wandering; it has form and direction. It is directing our attention to a specific area of interest. **Scripture meditation is thinking with intention.**

Scripture meditation need not be a solemn, academic exercise. It helps to have an attitude of curiosity and expectation, which lead to exciting discoveries, a refreshed spirit, and transformation of our thinking and behavior. It brings reward and benefit. It is a crucial step toward fully knowing and obeying God's will.

Here are three methods of meditation you can try that will enable you to grow in this discipline.

1. Paraphrase. Some exciting insights can come from rewriting a verse or passage in your own words. By restating a passage in your own words, you are required to think of accurate synonyms and phrases that express the thought of the passage, thus enabling you to better grasp its meaning.

For instance, Isaiah 26:3 reads, "Thou dost keep him in perfect peace, whose mind is stayed on thee, because he trusts in thee." A paraphrase of this verse might read, "You promise freedom from worry to the person who trust you completely, without any doubts in his mind."

2. Ask Questions. You can explore a verse more thoroughly by asking *who, what, when, where, why,* and *how* questions, or by jotting down random questions that come to your mind as you memorize and reflect on it. Questions such as, "What is this verse not saying?" or "What would be the opposite of this thought?" or "Where do I see myself in this passage?" are also helpful.

For instance, after reading Isaiah 26:3, you could ask, "To *Whom* does God give perfect peace?" "*What* is involved in 'staying' my mind on God?" or "*Why* would someone avoid Christ's provision for this peace?"

3. Pray. Memorizing a verse is helpful, meditating on a verse is great, but praying over or through the phrases of a verse anchors it deeply in our soul. Thinking about a verse and finding in it things for which to praise and adore the Lord, or discussing with the Lord concepts, questions, and instructions, makes a verse come alive and contributes greatly to a changed life.

For instance we could read Isaiah 26:3 and praise and adore the Lord for his attribute of peace, a fruit of his Spirit, and honor him for his concern that we live and dwell in peace. We could confess our spirit of worry and agitation and discuss with him the cause of our anxiety and ask him for insight on how to become a trusting, worry-free Christian. Or we could intercede for people and situations that we are aware of where peace does not reign.

These methods of meditation on Scripture take us deeper into the meaning and implications of the passages we are committing to memory. They enable us to go back again and again to the same passage and receive additional nourishment. Meditation enhances the joy and nourishment that comes from sacred Scripture and makes the work of committing passages to memory worthwhile.

Topic: Sin's Penalty

Verses: Romans 6:23 and Hebrews 9:27

Your Plan This Week

1. Read "How to Meditate on the Scriptures" on page 38, and place a check here when you have completed reading it.

   _____

2. DAILY REVIEW: Review Series A, plus the first two verses in Series B.

Reflection on the Wisdom of the Church

Following St. Paul, the Church has always thought that the overwhelming misery which oppresses men and their inclination toward evil and death cannot be understood apart from their connection with Adam's sin and the fact that he has transmitted to us a sin with which we are all born afflicted, a sin which is the "death of the soul".[1]

Herein is mankind's dilemma: having sinned we must face both death and judgment. The Church teaches that death was "contrary to the plans of God the Creator and entered the world as a consequence of sin."[2] In addition, the Church teaches "there is no repentance for men after death,"[3] so our eternal destiny must be settled in this life. It is this consequence and fear of death which grips our hearts early in life and is caused by our "disobedience toward and lack of trust in God's goodness." Jesus died to remove this fear.

Many non-Christians do not have to be convinced of this dilemma because they are aware of and are concerned about it. Others, though aware of their guilt, try to ignore it by whistling in the dark and hoping that the consciousness of this impending encounter with death will just go away. But it won't. The Church teaches that "death entered the world on account of man's sin. Even though man's nature is mortal, God had destined him not to die. Death was therefore contrary to the plans of God the Creator and entered the world as a consequence of sin."[4] Little do they realize that this knowledge of death and judgment can be a good thing if it impels them to seek the Divine Remedy, Jesus, who was the death of death.

Questions for Meditation

Romans 6:23 (For context, read Romans 6:19–23)

- What purpose precedes St. Paul's recording of this verse?
- What is the difference between a wage and a gift?
- Describe in your own words what man earns for sin?
- How does the gift of eternal life come to us?

Hebrews 9:27 (For context, read Hebrews 9:24–28)

- How do you feel about death and judgment?
- How do you think non-Christians who do not have the hope of salvation deal with this eventuality?
- How does Jesus' sacrifice of himself affect each person's judgment day?

Notes

[1] *Catechism of the Catholic Church* 403
[2] *Ibid*,1008
[3] *Ibid*,393
[4] *Ibid,* 1008

Topic: Christ Paid the Penalty

Verses: Romans 5:8 and 1 Peter 3:18

Your Plan This Week

1. Follow the pattern for memorizing verses which you learned previously. Memorize the first new verse during the first two days of the week, and memorize the second new verse on days three and four.

2. DAILY REVIEW: Series A, plus the first four verses in Series B.

Reflection on the Wisdom of the Church

Having become conscious of our sinfulness and aware of its penalty, we can become overwhelmed with fear and regret, facing a dilemma for which we have no remedy. But the Good News is "No sin is too big: a finite wretchedness, however immense, can always be covered by an infinite mercifulness."[1]

As God's Son and our Savior, Jesus chose to endure the abuse of a sham interrogation and trial, and the cruel agony of crucifixion. It was out of love that the Father offered his Son in our stead, the Just for the unjust. It was out of love that the Son sacrificed his life, even though we were estranged from him. This overwhelming dread of death, the consequence of sin, was swallowed up by the death of Jesus.

> *This sacrifice of Christ is unique; … First, it is a gift from God the Father himself, for the Father handed his Son over to sinners in order to reconcile us with himself. At the same time it is the offering of the Son of God made man, who in freedom and love offered his life to his Father through the Holy Spirit in reparation for our disobedience.*[2]

That which Christ received we deserve, and the penalty we deserve to receive he paid in full. "In him, and only in him, are we set free from all alienation and doubt, from slavery to the power of sin and death."[3] Like the two thieves crucified with Jesus, we have choices. We can either recognize and accept his payment on our behalf, or we can choose to go it alone and end up paying the penalty in eternity. The Good News is that he has paid the penalty for us.

Questions for Meditation

Romans 5:8 (For context, read Romans 5:6–11)

- From this passage, how would you describe true love?

- What is the significance of God's loving us while we were still sinners?

- How would you define reconciliation?

1 Peter 3:18 (For context, read 1 Peter 3:17–22)

- Of what should we be reminded when we suffer unjustly?

- How does this verse describe the comprehensiveness of Christ's sacrifice?

- How does this verse relate to Jesus' cry on the cross, recorded in Matthew 27:46?

- How is our understanding of Baptism affected by this passage?

Notes

---

[1] Pope John Paul I from *Illustrissimi: Letters from Pope John Paul I*, page 25
[2] *Catechism of the Catholic Church* 614
[3] Pope John Paul II in *Mission of the Redeemer*, 11

Topic: Unmerited Salvation

Verses: Ephesians 2:8–9 and Titus 3:5

Your Plan This Week

1. Follow the pattern you learned previously for memorizing these verses.

2. DAILY REVIEW: Series A, plus the first six verses in Series B.

Reflection on the Wisdom of the Church

Is there anything we can say or do that might offset our offenses toward God and gain us entrance into heaven? That is the issue we need to address with well-meaning people who are relying on their own righteousness for salvation. For many think their eternal destiny is determined by a great heavenly scale which weighs our good deeds against the wrongs we have committed. They think if the good outweighs the bad, then maybe they just might make it to heaven.

Sacred Scripture and the Church emphatically say this is not true.

Since the initiative belongs to God in the order of grace, no one can merit the initial grace of forgiveness and justification, at the beginning of conversion.[1]

By giving up his own Son for our sins, God manifests that his plan for us is one of benevolent love, prior to any merit on our part:...[2]

Thus, we can affirm with Pope John Paul II that "our faith in Christ, the one Savior of humanity, a faith we have received as a gift from on high, not as a result of any merit of our own."[3] For the majority of mankind this is the message of hope they are longing to hear.

To the self-sufficient, to those who do not wish to acknowledge the penalty God says they deserve, this is not good news. Though well-meaning, they are trying to warrant their salvation rather than rely on Christ's sufficiency. Pope Clement I (later elevated to sainthood) makes clear that this cannot be so: "We are not justified by our wisdom, intelligence, piety, or by any action of ours, however holy, but by faith, the one means by which God has justified men from the beginning."[4] **The Good News we carry to others includes the truth that we cannot and no longer need to try and earn our salvation.**

Questions for Meditation

Ephesians 2:8–9 (For context, read Ephesians 2:4–10)

- How would you define grace? Faith? Gift?
- In the context of Ephesians would you describe works as a cause or an effect of salvation?
- How should knowing the truths of verse 10 affect the way you live out your salvation?

Titus 3:5 (For context, read Titus 3:5–8)

- On whom are the kindness of Jesus and the gift of salvation bestowed?
- How is the *gift* of salvation described in this passage?
- How would someone manifest that he is relying on his works of righteousness to save himself?
- On the basis of these two memory verses, write a simple mission statement for a Christian.

Notes

[1] *Catechism of the Catholic Church* 2010
[2] Ibid, 604
[3] *Mission of the Redeemer,* by Pope John Paul II (11)
[4] Saint Clement I, pope, from, LOH, Vol. III, page 76

Topic: Personal Response

Verses: John 1:12 and Romans 10:9–10

Your Plan This Week

1. Remember to follow the daily plan for memorizing your new verses.

2. DAILY REVIEW: Series A, plus the first eight verses in Series B.

Reflection on the Wisdom of the Church

Rightly does the Church talk about the *mystery* of salvation, for many would, if they had their way, take all of the mystery out of salvation, analyze it, codify it, and market it as the only formula that will get anyone to heaven. Our focus should not be so much on the *how* of one's personal response to God but on the *necessity* of it.

Additionally, the Church refers to the *gift* of salvation as a gift freely given and which needs to be freely received.

> *"Salvation consists in believing and accepting the mystery of the Father and of his love, made manifest and freely given in Jesus through the Spirit."*[1]

Though it can be received on our behalf while we are yet infants, the Church teaches that upon maturing, we must confirm acceptance of the *gift* of salvation by a personal response. Pope Paul VI refers to this personal decision as "a radical conversion, a profound change of mind and heart."[2] Pope John Paul II further explains that "Conversion means accepting, by a personal decision, the saving sovereignty of Christ and becoming his disciple."[3]

How we express that personal response of belief in the saving work of Christ varies greatly and is dependent on many factors: our age, the amount of instruction we have received, our temperament, the environment in which we heard the Good News, etc. But however our faith is expressed, it always involves the heart and the willful confession before others that Jesus is both Savior and Lord and includes our intent to become his disciple.

Questions for Meditation

John 1:12 (For context, read John 1:8–13)

- To whom does God give the right to become his children?

- How are the words "received" and "believe" similar or different?

- There are many ways a person can express his personal response of faith. Describe your experience of personal response.

Romans 10:9,10 (For context, read Romans 10:6–13)

- How does this verse point out that faith is more than mere intellectual assent?

- Why are both belief and confession necessary for salvation?

- Explain whether this passage describes a one-time initial response, an ongoing process, or both.

Notes

---

[1] *Mission of the Redeemer* by Pope John Paul II, paragraph 12
[2] *On Evangelization In The Modern World* by Pope Paul VI, paragraph 9–10
[3] *Mission of the Redeemer* by Pope John Paul II, paragraph 46)

Topic: Assurance of God's Mercy

Verses: Philippians 1:6 and 1 John 5:13

▶ Your Plan This Week

DAILY REVIEW: Series A, plus all the verses in Series B.

▶ Reflection on the Wisdom of the Church

God does not want us to go through life worrying about our salvation, nor does he want us to go through life overconfidently thinking that our eternal destiny rests *solely* on some past response to God. The former can make us fearful and keep us from focusing on the joy of our salvation and growth in Christ and/or cause us to try and earn that which is truly a gift. The latter condition can make us presumptuous and oblivious to the consequences of our actions, or oblivious to Jesus' warnings, like in Matthew 24:13 where Jesus cautions that people will grow cold in their love for God, "But he who endures to the end will be saved."

The key to assurance of our salvation is not to look to ourselves but to Jesus.

> *Let us also lay aside every weight and sin which clings so closely, and let us run with perseverance the race that is set before us, looking to Jesus the pioneer and perfecter of our faith, who for the joy that was set before him endured the cross, despising the shame, and is seated at the right hand of the throne of God.[1]*

As we continue to love and follow Christ, we can be free of fear and confident in his mercy and faithfulness to bring us to eternal life—we should never doubt that he is utterly reliable. As St. Cyril tells us:

> *How great is God's love for men! Some good men have been found pleasing to God because of years of work. What they achieved by working for many hours at a task pleasing to God is freely given to you by Jesus in one short hour. For if you believe that Jesus Christ is Lord and that God raised him from the dead, you will be saved and taken up to paradise by him, just as he brought the thief there. Do not doubt that this is possible. After all, he saved the thief on the holy hill of Golgotha because of one hour's faith; will he not save you too since you have believed?[2]*

Questions for Meditation

Philippians 1:6 (For context, read Philippians 1:3–11)

- From where or whom do you think the writer of Philippians got his confidence?

- Whom was he relying on to insure the Philippians' final salvation?

- What responsibilities did the Philippians have in verses 9–11?

- To what extent do you see God perfecting your life in Christ?

1 John 5:13 (For context, read 1 John 5:10–15)

- What was John's primary objective in writing these words?

- What or whom should we rely on when we doubt what Christ has done for us?

- What are some of the reasons people lose confidence in their salvation?

- On what or in whom does this confidence reside?

Notes

---

[1] Hebrews 12:1–2
[2] Saint Cyril of Jerusalem, from catechetical instruction, LOH, Vol. IV, Page 484

Topic: Be Baptized

Verses: Acts 2:38 and Galatians 3:26–27

▶ **Your Plan This Week**

DAILY REVIEW: Series A, plus all the verses in Series B.

▶ **Reflection on the Wisdom of the Church**

From the earliest days of the Church, believers have affirmed the necessity of baptism. In Jesus' final days with his disciples, he left them a commission which we cannot ignore, a commission which included baptism: "Go therefore and make disciples of all nations, *baptizing them in the name of the Father and of the Son and of the Holy Spirit,* teaching them to observe all that I have commanded you…" (Matthew 28:19–20). Baptism is a sacrament which he commanded to be observed and which historically enabled a person to publicly identify with the death, burial, and resurrection of Jesus, as well as to gain entrance into the community of faith.

> *From the time of the apostles, becoming a Christian has been accomplished by a journey and initiation in several stages. This journey can be covered rapidly or slowly, but certain essential elements will always have to be present: proclamation of the Word, acceptance of the Gospel entailing conversion, profession of faith, Baptism itself, the outpouring of the Holy Spirit, and admission to Eucharistic communion.[1]*

It is interesting that believers were to be baptized in the name of the Father, Son, and Holy Spirit. When a person is adopted, they have the right to take the name of the adopting family. In a similar way, God desires that all people should become baptized into his family and bear the name of the Triune God for all time. With this privilege comes the responsibility of family membership and sharing in the family's purpose and tasks. One of these is the task of evangelization. Evangelization has as its rightful end the birthing and baptism of new believers and their incorporation into the local Eucharistic community. There, one's life of discipleship can be nurtured and a person can take his rightful place in the task of evangelization, thus living out his baptismal vows.

Questions for Meditation

Acts 2:38 (For context, read Acts 2:37–42)

- How significant is it to your understanding of the importance of baptism that the first sermon by the apostles (Peter in this case) called for repentance and baptism?

- What is the promise Saint Peter refers to in verse 39?

- How did these new believers live out their baptismal vows?

- Define what is meant by the word "devoted."

Galatians 3:26–27 (For context, read Galatians 3:19–29)

- What are the two operative actions in these verses?

- What part is ours and what part is God's?

- According to this passage, what change takes place in us through faith and baptism?

- Describe what it means to be "clothed with Christ".

The more meaningful a verse is to you, the easier it is to remember. That's why it is important to read each verse in its context and understand it before you memorize it. You will also want to pray about the things mentioned in the verse.

Notes

---

[1] *Catechism of the Catholic Church,* 1229

Rely on God's Resources

According to 2 Peter 1:3, God has given to us everything we need for life and for godliness "through the knowledge of him who called us to his own glory and excellence."

Knowing our limitations and the tests and trials that we will encounter, the Lord has provided the resources we need to live our lives consistent with his will and in a way that pleases him. These resources are intimately connected to Christ. The resource he has provided for us is Christ himself.

> He belongs to you, but more than that, he longs to be in you, living and ruling in you, as the head lives and rules in the body. He desires that whatever is in him may live and rule in you: his breath in your breath, his heart in your heart, all the faculties of his soul in the faculties of your soul, so that these words may be fulfilled in you: Glorify God and bear him in your body, that the life of Jesus may be made manifest in you.[1]

We can avail ourselves of Christ's resources by utilizing three simple steps, which Saint Paul tells us about in Colossians 3. He advises us to seek the things above, or the things of God in Christ, and to set our minds on these things. Saint Paul understood that the spiritual battle begins with the mind and so advises us to focus our minds on Christ. When we consistently do that, we are slowly transformed into his image.

The next two steps should take place simultaneously. Saint Paul uses the metaphor of taking off our old clothes and putting on new clothes. By this he means for us to abandon our old ways of thinking and replace them with attitudes and behavior that is consistent with Christ's character and will. This process of transformation *from the inside out* is made possible only in Christ and through the resources he provides.

Series C: Rely on God's Resources identifies seven spiritual resources Christ provides so you can find the means to love God and do his will. Each of these resources is vitally important and a source of hope.

His Spirit—John 14:26 and 1 Corinthians 2:12
His Presence—1 Corinthians 10:16 and John 6:55–56
His Strength—Isaiah 41:10 and Philippians 4:13
His Faithfulness—Lamentations 3:22–23 and Numbers 23:19
His Peace—Isaiah 26:3 and 1 Peter 5:7
His Provision—Ephesians 6:10–11 and Philippians 4:19
His Help in Temptation—Hebrews 2:18 and 1 Corinthians 10:13

---

[1] From a treatise by Saint John Eudes, as found in LOH, Vol. IV, page 1331

Topic: His Spirit

Verses: John 14:26 and 1 Corinthians 2:12

▶ **Your Plan This Week**

1. With daily practice, you already have learned important principles for effective Scripture memory and review. Continue to build these habits into your life. You may want to review "Principles for Memorizing Scripture" on page 11.

2. For the remaining weeks of this course, remember to follow the weekly plan that you have learned for memorizing the two new verses.

3. DAILY REVIEW: All the verses in Series B.

▶ **Reflection on the Wisdom of the Church**

The Scripture speaks of walking (living) in the flesh and walking (living) in the Spirit. When most of us think of living in the flesh, we usually understand this to mean issues of immorality, carnality, and illicit sexuality. But it is more complex than that. Very moral and upright Christian church-goers can live the majority of their lives in the flesh by simply being self-willed and self-reliant. On the other hand, living in the Spirit need not be thought of as a super-spiritual or mystical experience when it is simply conscious awareness of the Holy Spirit, submission to his will, and reliance on his help.

Christ has given us no greater resource than the Holy Spirit. So great is this resource that Jesus said, "it is to your advantage that I go away, for if I do not go away, the Counselor will not come to you" (John 14:16). The Holy Spirit provides enlightenment to our mind and strengthens our will to understand and respond to the Gospel. He affirms our faith by sealing our salvation with his presence and making us receptive to renewal and transformation. He imbues us with the fruit of his presence and gifts us to be responsible stewards in Christ's mission.

> *The Spirit comes with the tenderness of a true friend and protector to save, to heal, to teach, to counsel, to strengthen, to console. The Spirit comes to enlighten the mind first of the one who receives him, and then, through him, the minds of others as well.*[1]

We would do well to follow the advice Pope John Paul II's father gave him, which was to begin each day praying, "Come, Holy Spirit."

Questions for Meditation

John 14:26 (For context, read John 14:21–27)

- Where do you see evidence for the Trinity in this passage?
- What does the name "Counselor" communicate to you?
- What other names for the Holy Spirit are you aware of?
- How are the Holy Spirit's actions in this verse valuable to the Church and the individual?

1 Corinthians 2:12 (For context, read 1 Corinthians 2:6–16)

- From where or from whom comes spiritual insight and wisdom?
- How do we either cooperate with the Holy Spirit or resist him in coming to know the things given to us of God?
- How would you describe your attentiveness to the Holy Spirit?
- How can you increase your sensitivity to him?

Notes

---

[1] From a catechetical instruction by Saint Cyril of Jerusalem, LOH Vol. II, page 968

Topic: His Presence

Verses: 1 Corinthians 10:16 and John 6:55–56

Your Plan This Week

1. Don't be overwhelmed by your daily review. Most people can review their verses at a rate of 3–4 verses a minute once they have learned them well. Thus, reviewing the entire 14 verses of a series should only take a few minutes.

2. DAILY REVIEW: Review all the verses in Series B, plus the first two verses in Series C.

Reflection on the Wisdom of the Church

Vatican II makes clear that one of our greatest resources is Christ's presence. The Council pointed out that in addition to Jesus' presence in the Eucharist, he is also present in the Word when the Scripture is read; in his people when they gather to sing and worship; in the liturgy and sacraments; and in the person of his minister. However, in the midst of these many ways in which Jesus is present to us, the Church teaches that in a unique way, Jesus' presence in the Eucharist is "the source and summit of the Christian life."[1] Consequently, our commitment to regularly participate in the sacrament of receiving Christ in the Eucharist is one of the essential ways in which we rely on *his* resources. In addition, Vatican II explains:

> The Church has received the Eucharist from Christ her Lord not as one gift—however precious—among so many others, but as the gift par excellence, for it is the gift of himself, of his person in his sacred humanity, as well as the gift of his saving work. Nor does it remain confined to the past, since "all that Christ is—all that he did and suffered for all men—participates in the divine eternity, and so transcends all times."[2]

The Eucharist memorializes *the central event* of our salvation and makes present to us again the one sacrifice of Christ on the cross. Rightly do we see why it is called *the source* of our Christian life. Inasmuch as Christ's sacrifice makes communion with himself, the Father and the Holy Spirit possible, it is the goal and *summit* of our salvation.

> Blessed is the man who, whenever he celebrates the Eucharist or receives Communion, offers himself to Our Lord as a living sacrifice.[3]

Questions for Meditation

1 Corinthians 10:16 (For context, read 1 Corinthians 10:16; 11:23–29)

- From whom did Saint Paul claim to receive this sacrament?
- What did you learn in this passage about how you should receive Christ in the Eucharist?
- Of what is it a memorial?
- To what do verses 10:16 and 11:27 equate the Eucharist bread and drink?

John 6:55–56 (For context, read John 6:51–58)

- What evidence is there in this passage that Jesus was not speaking figuratively?
- Jesus likens his presence in the Eucharist to real food and drink. What does food and drink do for our lives?
- What does the word "abide" mean (vs. 56)?
- List the promises connected with eating Jesus' body and drinking his blood.

Notes

---

[1] Catechism of the Catholic Church, 1324.
[2] *On the Eucharist in Its Relationship to the Church,* by Pope John Paul II, 11.
[3] *The Imitation of Christ,* by Thomas á Kempis, page 203.

Topic: His Strength

Verses: Isaiah 41:10 and Philippians 4:13

Your Plan This Week

1. Once you learn the verses for this topic, you will be halfway through the *Catholic Topical Memory System*. To review what you have learned about Scripture memory principles so far, take the self-checking quiz on page 62.

2. DAILY REVIEW: Series B, plus the first four verses in Series C.

Reflection on the Wisdom of the Church

In 1 Thessalonians 5:24, Saint Paul says, "He who calls you is faithful, and he will do it." God does not ask us to do anything for which he will not give us the strength. History bears this out as we look at the great saints of the Church and the martyrs who willingly gave their lives out of love for Christ and for his glory.

Most of us, though, will never be called upon to be martyrs. For us, the issue is having the courage and strength to live each day aware of his presence and yielded to his will. Saint Francis de Sales reminds us,

> *"Humility believes that it can do nothing, considering its poverty and weakness, if we depend on ourselves. On the contrary, generosity makes us say with St. Paul, 'I can do all things in Him who strengthens me.' Humility makes us mistrust ourselves; generosity makes us trust in God."*[1]

We can rely on his strength to equip us to do his will, when we desire it.

Christ's strength comes to us primarily through the indwelling of the Holy Spirit. The Holy Spirit can and will provide unique strength in unusual and unique situations, as he has for people like Christian martyrs. However, the normal way he does this is by enabling us to mature and grow in a healthy and strong manner. In several places, sacred Scripture uses the metaphor of a tree to describe the normative strengthening and well-being that comes from relying on him: with its roots tapping into a rich source of nourishment, the tree is able to remain not only strong but also fruitful in the midst of draught (Ps 1:3). We can be nourished by him as we read the Scripture, pray, unite with his people, and avail ourselves of his presence in the liturgy and sacraments.

Questions for Meditation

Isaiah 41:10 (For context, Isaiah 41:8–14)

- What promises does God give to Israel in these verses?

- What does this passage reveal about the kind of relationship God wants to have with his people?

- To what extent can you draw on the truths of this passage?

Philippians 4:13 (For context, Philippians 4:10–19)

- What are some situations in your life where you need to rely on God's strength?

- How does this memory verse relate to Saint Paul's statement about learning to be content (Philippians 4:11)?

- How can we become a vehicle of God's strength for people who are experiencing hunger, suffering, and affliction, as Saint Paul did?

Notes

---

[1] *The Art of Loving God,* by St. Francis de Sales, from Conference V, page 29

Topic: His Faithfulness

Verses: Lamentations 3:22–23 and Numbers 23:19

Your Plan This Week

1. Using your spare moments will take the stress out of daily review, as well as help anchor your thoughts on Christ throughout the day.

2. DAILY REVIEW: Series B, plus the first six verses in Series C. Also, review all of Series A at least once this week.

Reflection on the Wisdom of the Church

The strength of our faith is dependent upon the extent to which we believe that God is faithful. Will he do what he says he will do? Will he consistently remain true to his character? Will his love and commitment to us never fail? Unless we can answer a resounding "Yes!" to these and similar types of questions, our faith and commitment will be weak, and we will "hedge our bets," just in case God fails.

But it is not within God's nature to be fickle, capricious, and unreliable, for as God says, "I the LORD do not change; therefore you, O sons of Jacob, are not consumed" (Malachi 3:6). His love is constant, his word is constant, and his nature varies not. When we awake tomorrow we will find him as he was today—utterly reliable. "He is ever the same and unchanging, deceiving neither in his essence nor in his promise. As again says the apostle writing to the Thessalonians, 'Faithful is he who calls you, who also will do it;' for in doing what he promises, he is faithful to his words."[1]

As we come to increasingly believe that he is utterly reliable, anxiety will begin to flee and we will discover, as did Saint Elizabeth Seton, that God is faithful to guide, to meet our every need, and to lovingly care for us.

And in every disappointment, great or small, let your dear heart fly direct to Him, your dear Savior, throwing yourself in His arms for refuge against every pain and sorrow. He never will leave you or forsake you.[2]

Questions for Meditation

Lamentations 3:22–23 (For context, read Lamentations 3:19–32)

- What enabled Jeremiah to wait and endure in hope during the difficult times of his life?

- What examples of God's faithfulness have you seen in your life?

Numbers 23:19 (For context, read Numbers 23:13–26)

- How can the truth of this passage increase your faith?

- How would you restate this verse in your own words?

- Describe the difference between "waiting on the Lord" and stoic endurance?

- Practically, how can we increase our ability to recognize and recall the Lord's loving kindnesses to us?

Notes

---

[1] Saint Athanasius in a Treatise Against the Arians, from *Ancient Christian Commentary on Scripture,* Vol IX, page 246

[2] Saint Elizabeth Seton from *The Soul of Elizabeth Seton,* page 64

This quiz will help you check your understanding of Scripture memory principles. After answering the questions, compare your answers with those listed at the end of the quiz.

1. Your success in memorizing Scripture depends entirely on your own ability and confidence. (Circle your answer)

   ☐ TRUE   ☐ FALSE

2. Learning the topics with the verses ... (Check the best answer)

   ☐ a. Is optional in the Topical Memory System.

   ☐ b. Gives you mental hooks with which you can draw a particular verse from memory when you need it.

   ☐ c. Is a good mental exercise because it makes learning the verses more difficult.

3. It is best to learn the verses by heart because this ... (Check the best answers.)

   ☐ a. Will give you greater confidence in using your verses.

   ☐ b. Makes it easier to learn verses initially and to review them later.

   ☐ c. Impresses others with your knowledge of Scripture.

4. The verses in Series A deal with the essential elements of the obedient, Christ–centered life. (Circle your answer)

   ☐ TRUE   ☐ FALSE

5. In which aspect of the Christian life are the verses in Series B most helpful?

   ☐ a. Knowing the will of God.

   ☐ b. Fellowship.

   ☐ c. Knowing how to witness to others.

   ☐ d. Knowing how to overcome anxiety.

   ☐ e. Prayer.

6. Why is it helpful to memorize and review Scripture with one or more friends? (Check the *three* best answers.)

   ☐ a. It provides mutual encouragement.

   ☐ b. You can show others how well you are doing.

   ☐ c. It provides opportunities to discuss difficulties in memorization.

□ d. It allows you to compare yourself with others.

□ e. You have someone with whom to share how God is using the verses in your life.

7. A first step toward knowing and obeying God's will is to ... (Check the correct answer.)

□ a. Straighten out your life as best you can.

□ b. Know a lot about the Bible.

□ c. Meditate on sacred Scripture.

8. Two essentials for a successful Scripture memory program are ... (Circle the *two* best answers.)

- Jotting down references of verses you want to learn later.

- Marking memorized verses in your Bible.

- Consistently memorizing new verses each week.

- Following a regular, daily program of reviewing verses you dhave learned.

9. If memorizing new verses ever becomes routine or lifeless, these things could be done: (Circle the *two* best answers.)

- Stop memorizing for a month or six weeks.

- Spend more time praying over and meditating on your verses

- Find a new way of memorizing.

- Begin using the verses in conversation and in writing.

10. Indicate with letters (A–E) the proper order of the five series of verses in the Catholic Topical Memory System.

_____ Rely on God's Resources

_____ Grow in Christlikeness

_____ Proclaim Christ

_____ Live the New Life

_____ Be Christ's Disciple

Correct Answers:

1. FALSE	6. A, C and E
2. B	7. C
3. A and B	8. C and D
4. TRUE	9. B and D
5. C	10. C, E, B, A and D

Topic: His Peace

Verses: Isaiah 26:3 and 1 Peter 5:7

▶ **Your Plan This Week**

DAILY REVIEW: Series B, plus the first eight verses in Series C.

▶ **Reflection on the Wisdom of the Church**

"Be not afraid" was the message of Pope John Paul II in 1978 at his inaugural, a time in which there was much to be afraid of which could disturb our peace and the peace of the world. His solution was simple: "Open wide the doors for Christ," a message he faithfully restated in many ways during his pontificate. Fear causes us to close in on ourselves, lock the doors and close the windows of our soul. Peace, *God's peace*, removes that fear and calms our heart as we open wide the doors to our soul for Christ to enter and dispel our fear.

In Scripture, God is sometimes called 'the God of peace' (Romans 15:33). Jesus is referred to as 'the Lord of peace' (2 Thessalonians 3:16), and the prophet Isaiah, speaking about the coming Messiah, calls him the 'Prince of Peace' (Isaiah 9:6). Peace has several dimensions: peace in our relationship with God; inner peace within our hearts and minds; and peace with our fellow human beings. These three areas of peace are interconnected. Peace with God leads us to inner peace, which in turn overflows to peaceful relationships with others.

> *Peace needn't be elusive; it is a gift Jesus bequeaths to us. 'Peace I leave with you; my peace I give to you' (John 14:27). Peace is a gift that resides in Jesus and comes to us through the Holy Spirit as we learn to trust the Father as Jesus did. Peace requires that we hear the message of the risen Lord, 'Do not be afraid' (Matthew 28:10), with the inner ear of our heart.* [1]

Let us pray with Saint Thomas á Kempis, "Grant me, above all else, to rest in You, that my heart may find its peace in You alone; for You are the heart's true peace, its sole abiding place, and outside Yourself all is hard and restless." [2]

Questions for Meditation

Isaiah 26:3 (For context, read Isaiah 26:1–10,12)

- What can we learn about trusting God from Israel's experience?

- How does the truth of this verse relate to Philippians 4:6–7?

- How can scripture memory enable you to keep your mind focused on Christ?

- In this passage, what effect does a mind focused on the Lord have on our behavior?

1 Peter 5:7 (For context, read 1 Peter 5:1–11)

- How does a person give their anxieties over to Christ?

- From the context of this verse, what is the relationship between humility and knowing God's peace?

- What principles in verses 8–10 should we be aware of that will help remove anxiety and contribute to our inner peace?

- What anxieties are you currently facing to which these truths can be applied?

Notes

---

[1] *Living in the Power of the Holy Spirit,* by Rich Cleveland, pages 61, 62
[2] Saint Thomas à Kempis, *Imitation of Christ,* Book 3, Chapter 15

Topic: His Provision

Verses: Ephesians 6:10–11 and Philippians 4:19

Your Plan This Week

1. Read "Two Essentials in Scripture Memory" and "If Your Scripture Memory Work Becomes Too Routine" on page 68 .

2. DAILY REVIEW: Series B, plus the first 10 verses in Series C.

Reflection on the Wisdom of the Church

The Father makes an interesting statement in Psalms 50:10–12: "Every beast of the forest is mine, the cattle on a thousand hills. I know all the birds of the air, and all that moves in the field is mine. If I were hungry, I would not tell you; for the world and all that is in it is mine." He ends this Psalm by telling the Israelites to offer him a "sacrifice of thanksgiving."

Giving thanks to God forces us to focus on his current and past provision for us, which in turn gives us hope that he will continue to provide for us in the future. One of our problems is that we often do not accurately assess the current state of God's provision for us. Because we work hard or are talented, we often mistakenly believe that our own hands have provided for our needs, when in reality, he is the one who enables and the one who blesses our work and talents.

God provides for us in many wonderful ways. Sometimes it is by giving us the talent and energy we spoke of above. Sometimes he provides through other members of the Body of Christ. Paul, reminding us that Christ became poor that we might become rich, points out that one means of God's provision is the generosity of those who have resources:

> For if the readiness is there, it is acceptable according to what a man has, not according to what he has not. I do not mean that others should be eased and you burdened, but that as a matter of equality your abundance at the present time should supply their want, so that their abundance may supply your want, that there may be equality.[1]

Additionally the Bible is full of stories where God provided in extraordinary ways also, when there were extraordinary needs. This is one of the advantages of regular, daily reading of the Old and New Testaments: they enable us to get a fresh picture of God's extraordinary love and provision for his people. These biblical accounts remind us that God is infinitely able and willing to meet his people's needs. He still is able to do extraordinary things when needed;

however, most of us simply need to recognize and give thanks for God's provision in the ordinary aspects of our lives.

Questions for Meditation

Ephesians 6:10–11 (For context, Ephesians 6:10–20)

- What are some ways in which God provides for our needs?
- Briefly state in your own words the following statements:
  - "Girded your loins with truth"
  - "Put on the breastplate of righteousness"
  - "Shod your feet with the equipment of the gospel of peace"
  - "Taking the shield of faith"
  - "Take the helmet of salvation"
  - "Sword of the Spirit"
- Practically, how can we put on these provisions?

Philippians 4:19 (For context, Philippians 4:10–20)

- What is the difference between a need and a desire?
- What attitudes and experiences preceded Paul's statement of confidence in God's provision?
- Where does God's provision for our needs reside?

Notes

---

[1] 2 Corinthians 8:12–14

Two Essentials in Scripture Memory

Two rules form the foundation for a successful Scripture memory program:

1. *Consistently memorize new verses each week.*

2. *Follow a regular, daily program of reviewing the verses you have already memorized*

If at the end of a particular week you cannot quote the verses you intended to memorize that week, you may be tempted to think, *I won't memorize any new verses next week, but instead will concentrate on learning these before resuming work on new verses.*

But skipping one week makes it easier to skip another, and then another. Instead, you should memorize new verses as usual, and put extra effort into learning any verses you have missed. Ask for God's help!

If Your Scripture Memory Work Becomes Too Routine

Don't get discouraged! The process of recording Scripture on your mind and heart does have a mechanical aspect. It requires certain repetitive methods and a great deal of perseverance. But as long as the process of imprinting God's word on your heart is moving forward, these Scriptures will be continually available for life-giving work.

There are helpful things you can do if your Scripture memory program seems lifeless. Try spending more time going over your verses in prayer and meditation. Also begin using the verses in your conversations and in prayer. New freshness can come through sharing the Scriptures with others.

Keep in mind that memorizing and meditating on sacred Scripture is a practical way of making them available for the Holy Spirit to use in your life.

Topic: His Help in Temptation
Verses: Hebrews 2:18 and 1 Corinthians 10:13

Your Plan This Week

DAILY REVIEW: Series B, plus the first 12 verses in Series C. Also, review all of Series A at least once this week.

Reflection on the Wisdom of the Church

Many of us suffer needlessly because we have not learned to differentiate between temptation and sin. Consequently, when we are tempted we often feel guilt and become discouraged, as though we had yielded to the temptation. Frequently, the discouragement and guilt then create a mental and emotional environment, which in turn makes yielding to the temptation that much easier. St. Francis de Sales advice is particularly pertinent on this point:

> *Temptation to a certain sin, to any sin whatsoever, might last throughout our whole life, yet it can never make us displeasing to God's Majesty, provided we do not take pleasure in it and give consent to it. The reason is that when we are tempted we are not active but passive and inasmuch as we do not take pleasure in it we cannot incur any guilt.*
>
> *...That is, we may feel temptations even though they displease us but we can never consent to them unless they please us, since to be pleased by them usually is a step toward consent to them. ... As long as we remain steadfast in our resolutions not to take pleasure in the temptation, it is utterly impossible for us to offend God,...[1]*

God will never abandon us in the midst of our temptations. Rather, he will faithfully provide us with the strength and means to escape their control. In keeping with this thought, we read the advice of Saint Thomas á Kempis: "We must not despair, therefore, when we are tempted, but earnestly pray God to grant us his help in every need."[2] And through the indwelling of Holy Spirit, that help will come.

Questions for Meditation

Hebrews 2:18 (For context, read Hebrews 2:10–18)

- What is the difference between temptation and sin?
- How does knowing that Jesus was also tempted affect your relationship with him?
- What is the purpose of Jesus' Incarnation and Passion?
- How many ways can you think of that Jesus aids those who are tempted?

1 Corinthians 10:13 (For context, read 1 Corinthians 10:7–14)

- Name at least three things this passage teaches about temptation.
- According to this passage, how can we increase our ability to withstand temptation?
- What does God desire regarding your struggles with sin?

Notes

---

[1] *Introduction to the Devout Life,* by Saint Francis de Sales, page 239, 240
[2] Saint Thomas à Kempis in, *Imitation of Christ,* Book 1, Chapter 13.

Be Christ's Disciple

Except for his redemptive work on the cross, one of Jesus Christ's most important works on earth was forming a band of dedicated disciples who would multiply and impact the world regarding the Kingdom of Heaven. Christ used these disciples to establish the Church, the Body of Christ.

Jesus ministered to the multitudes, but he was not simply interested in being popular with the people. He raised serious issues, asked hard questions, and required some difficult commitments. Jesus was not interested in producing nominal followers; he was interested in developing true, committed disciples who had counted the cost and on whom he could depend.

He is still looking for disciples who will follow him in joyful, wholehearted obedience, disciples who will be committed to the stewardship of all that he has entrusted to us. "Becoming a disciple of Jesus Christ leads naturally to the practice of stewardship. These linked realities, discipleship and stewardship, then make up the fabric of a Christian life in which each day is lived in an intimate, personal relationship with the Lord.

"Following Jesus is the work of a lifetime. At every step forward, one is challenged to go further in accepting and loving God's will. Being a disciple is not just something else to do, alongside many other things suitable for Christians, it is a total way of life and requires continuing conversion."[1]

In these next seven topics and 14 verses, you will encounter various aspects of being Christ's disciple. Putting these concepts into practice may be viewed by some as the hard part, but in reality, they are the rewarding part and are the keys to true freedom and new life in Christ.

Series D: Be Christ's Disciple presents seven imperatives that characterize the kind of disciples Jesus seeks.

Put Christ First—Matthew 6:33 and Luke 9:23
Pursue Holiness—1 John 2:15–16 and Romans 12:1
Confess Sin—Psalm 32:5 and 1 John 1:9
Be Steadfast—1 Corinthians 15:58 and Hebrews 12:3
Serve Others—Mark 10:45 and Galatians 6:10
Give Generously—Proverbs 3:9–10 and 2 Corinthians 9:6–7
Develop World Vision—Acts 1:8 and Matthew 28:19–20

---

[1] *Stewardship A Disciples Response,* By National Council of Catholic Bishops, pages 13, 14.

Topic: Put Christ First

Verses: Matthew 6:33 and Luke 9:23

Your Plan This Week

1. Complete the topic and reference quiz on pages 75–76.

2. DAILY REVIEW: All of Series A and C.

Reflection on the Wisdom of the Church

There is no sadder person nor sadder Christian than the one who has decided to only go half-way with Christ. Partial commitment to Christ prevents a person from being able to enjoy the world, or enjoy being a Christian. Guilt and remorse follows their excursions into worldliness and sin, and when they are back among whole-hearted followers of Christ, they are racked with more remorse and guilt as they compare what they are with what they could be.

For the Christian, the way to happiness and fulfillment leads directly to the cross. Jesus said, "Whoever would **save** his life will lose it; and whoever loses his life for my sake, he will **save** it."

> *The full readiness to change — which might even better be termed readiness to become another man — is present in him only who, having heard the call 'Follow me' from the mouth of the Lord, follows Him as did the Apostles, leaving everything behind.' ... He is merely required to relinquish his old self, the natural foundation, and all purely natural standards, and open himself entirely to Christ's action.[1]...*

Saint Paul raises the issue of sin's continuing dominance over our lives in the face of our having received mercy and grace (Romans 7). He explains that sin should no longer have dominance over us and that the choice is ours. We can either "yield [our] members to sin as instruments of wickedness" or "yield [ourselves] to God as men (and women) who have been brought from death to life, and [our] members to God as instruments of righteousness." This is what is meant by putting God first.

Questions for Meditation

Matthew 6:33 (For context, read Matthew 6:25–34)

- In this passage, what are some of the things that might prevent a person from putting Christ first in his life?

- Which issues of life are most likely to hinder you from putting Christ first in your life?

- How would you define *righteousness* and *the Kingdom of God?* (You may want to use a standard dictionary, a Bible dictionary, or Bible encyclopedia to help define these terms.)

Luke 9:23 (For context, read Luke 9:18–27)

- From this passage, what seems to be the greatest hindrance to following Christ?

- How does this passage reflect the freedom of choice which the Lord gives us in deciding to follow him?

- What does Jesus mean by "take up your cross"?

- To what extent does our answer to Jesus' question, "Who do you say I am?" affect our willingness to follow Christ?

Notes

---

[1] *Transformation in Christ*, by Dietrich Von Hildebrand, page 8

For each of these topics in Series A, B, and C, fill in the blanks with the correct references.

A. Live the New Life (Write in the Bible reference below the topic.)

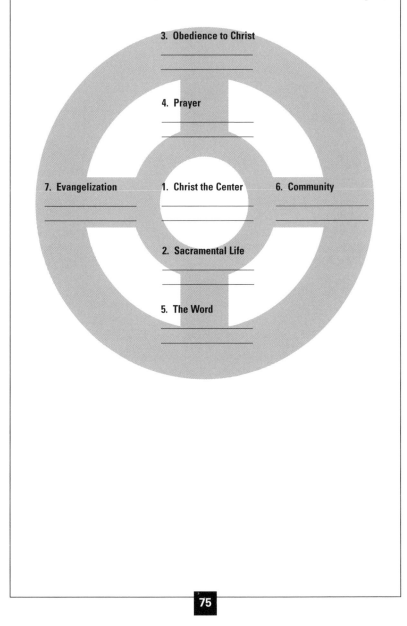

B. Proclaim Christ (Write in the Bible reference below the topic.)

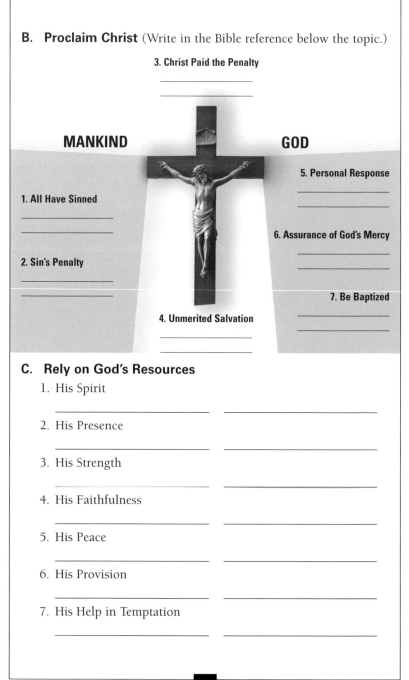

3. Christ Paid the Penalty

_____

_____

MANKIND

GOD

5. Personal Response

_____

_____

1. All Have Sinned

_____

_____

6. Assurance of God's Mercy

_____

_____

2. Sin's Penalty

_____

_____

7. Be Baptized

_____

4. Unmerited Salvation

_____

_____

C. Rely on God's Resources

1. His Spirit

_____   _____

2. His Presence

_____   _____

3. His Strength

_____   _____

4. His Faithfulness

_____   _____

5. His Peace

_____   _____

6. His Provision

_____   _____

7. His Help in Temptation

_____   _____

Topic: Pursue Holiness

Verses: 1 John 2:15–16 and Romans 12:1

Your Plan This Week

DAILY REVIEW: Series B and C, plus the first two verses in Series D.

Reflection on the Wisdom of the Church

God gives us the freedom to determine the direction of our lives. Pope John XXIII tells us that "Holiness consists not in penance and extraordinary practices but in seeking in all things the Lords will, in obedience and humility…"[1] Holiness is not simply performing a series of religious or spiritual disciplines; rather, it is using these disciplines to enable us to consciously and continually give our lives over to God's influence and will. As St. Gregory of Nyssa tells us,

> "All Christians in any state or walk of life are called to the fullness of Christian life and to the perfection of charity." All are called to holiness: "Be perfect, as your heavenly Father is perfect."

> In order to reach this perfection the faithful should use the strength dealt out to them by Christ's gift, so that … doing the will of the Father in everything, they may wholeheartedly devote themselves to the glory of God and to the service of their neighbor.[2]

Holiness, then, is not the absence of sin in a person's life but a condition of devoted-ness to the Lord. Some of the most holy saints were people very conscious of their sin and unworthiness. Rather, holiness is the setting aside or devoting of some thing totally to God. In this case, we are being called to be unconditionally devoted to God, or as one translation puts it, to be his "privately owned people". The one who is holy, set apart for God, is then naturally used to accomplish his will. As St. Gregory of Nyssa further explains, "the quality of holiness is shown not by what we say but by what we do in life."[3]

Questions for Meditation

1 John 2:15–16 (For context, read 1 John 2:12–17)

- How would you define "world" as it is used in this passage?

- From where or whom does "love for the world" come?

- According to this passage, what is necessary in life to enable us to be people who "renounce the world and its attractions"?

Romans 12:1 (For context, read Romans 11:32–12:2)

- What is the right motive for yielding ourselves to God?

- Describe what is meant by "a living sacrifice."

- How often is it necessary to make this dedication of our total being to God?

Notes

[1] Pope John XXIII in *I Will be Called John,* page 161
[2] *Catechism of the Catholic Church* 2013
[3] St. Gregory of Nyssa in the LOH, Vol. IV. Page 108

Topic: Confess Sin

Verses: Psalm 32:5 and 1 John 1:9

Your Plan This Week

DAILY REVIEW: Series B and C, plus the first four verses in Series D.

Reflection on the Wisdom of the Church

Participation in the Rite of Reconciliation is at once both a humbling and healing experience. Sacred Scripture says that "God resists the proud but *gives grace* to the humble," and those who avail themselves of the Sacrament of Reconciliation will attest to the grace received through the words of absolution.

> *Sin is before all else an offense against God, a rupture of communion with him. At the same time it damages communion with the Church. For this reason conversion entails both God's forgiveness and reconciliation with the Church, which are expressed and accomplished liturgically by the sacrament of Penance and Reconciliation.*

> *Only God forgives sins. Since he is the Son of God, Jesus says of himself, "the Son of man has authority on earth to forgive sins" and exercises this divine power: "Your sins are forgiven." Further, by virtue of his divine authority he gives this power to men to exercise in his name.*[1]

Christ's disciples should be faithful to deal with sin on a consistent basis. C.S. Lewis encourages us that *"No amount* of falls will really undo us if we keep picking ourselves up each time ... It is when we notice the dirt that God is most present in us: it is the very sign of His presence."[2] Consciousness of our sin should remind us of God's love. It is the Holy Spirit's gentle way of calling us to come in from the world and get cleaned up so we can once again go forth, fresh and clean and ready to represent the Savior. Each time we participate in the Sacrament of Reconciliation, it provides the opportunity to pick ourselves up, shake off the affects of sin, and begin again on the road to righteousness.

Questions for Meditation

Psalm 32:5 (For context, read Psalm 32:1–7)

- How does this Psalm describe the joy of forgiveness?
- What are the effects of choosing to not acknowledge one's sin?
- How does verse 5 define confession?
- How do you feel about acknowledging sin to another person and asking for forgiveness?
- How do you feel about regular participation in the Sacrament of Reconciliation?

1 John 1:9 (For context, read 1 John 1:5–2:2)

- Why does harboring sin within us contradict what being a Christian means?
- Describe how this passage reinforces the concept that sin affects our relationship with God and our relationship with fellow Christians (the Church).
- Explain what is meant by Jesus being an "advocate" and an "expiation for our sins."
- What is the good news of confession?

Notes

---

[1] *Catechism of the Catholic Church* 1440–1441
[2] CS Lewis in *The Inspirational Writings of CS Lewis, page* 296

Topic: Be Steadfast

Verses: 1 Corinthians 15:58 and Hebrews 12:3

▶ **Your Plan This Week**

DAILY REVIEW: Series B and C, plus the first six verses in Series D.

▶ **Reflection on the Wisdom of the Church**

One of the chief tactics of our enemy, Satan, is to destroy our will to continue on in obedience to Christ and in pursuit of his will. Quite often, Satan does this by trying to propel us down a path that begins with disappointment and escalates into a spiral of doubt, discouragement, depression, and eventually despair. We cannot avoid encountering disappointing situations or disappointing people, but we can nip this downward spiral in the bud by refusing to doubt God's love and purpose for our lives.

Another word for steadfastness is fortitude, "the courage to overcome the obstacles and difficulties that arise in the practice of our religious duties."[1] Isaiah 11:1–2 includes fortitude or steadfastness as one of the seven gifts of the Spirit which would rest upon the Messiah, and through his presence, upon his followers. It is in contemplating Christ's Passion, his endurance and steadfastness in the face of evil, that we gain strength to emulate him.

We see this reflected in the autobiography of Blessed Pope John XXIII. He tells us of the feelings he had to deal with in the latter days of his life when he was feeling the effects of old age and disease. "Sometimes the thought of the short time still left to me tempts me to slacken my efforts. But with God's help I will not give in. 'I neither fear to die nor refuse to live.' The Lord's will is still my peace."[2] What a marvelous testimony to the virtue of steadfastness! God has given us holy men and women, like Blessed Pope John XXIII, as examples from whom we can learn, and after whom we can model our lives. Let's pursue the virtue of steadfastness while whole and healthy so that if God calls us to endure sickness and infirmity in our latter years, we can do so with grace and purpose.

Questions for Meditation

1 Corinthians 15:58 (For context, read 1 Corinthians 15:50–58)

- Why do you think Christians need to be encouraged to persevere?

- How should our understanding of the perishable (temporal) and the imperishable (eternal) affect our steadfastness?

- What should give us confidence as we persevere in serving Christ?

Hebrews 12:3 (For context, read Hebrews 12:1–13)

- What keys to steadfast endurance do you see in this passage?

- What are some practical ways you can focus your thoughts on Jesus?

- What can be sources of weariness and faintheartedness?

- How does this passage encourage you to view difficulties?

Notes

[1] *Catholic Encyclopedia*
[2] Pope John XXIII in *Journal of a Soul,* page 284

Topic: Serve Others
Verses: Mark 10:45 and Galatians 6:10

Your Plan This Week

DAILY REVIEW: Series B and C, plus the first eight verses in Series D.

Reflection on the Wisdom of the Church

Jesus said there are no other commandments greater than these two: "You shall love the Lord your God with all your heart, and with all your soul, and with all your mind, and with all your strength," and "You shall love your neighbor as yourself" (Mark 12:30–31). Loving and serving others is the primary way we express that we wholeheartedly love God.

We are called the *Body* of Christ because it is through our physical beings that Jesus intends to encounter the peoples of the world. Our serving of others is simply his actions through us, and contrariwise, when we fail to serve others we limit his actions through us. Pope John Paul II points out that "Each Christian's words and life must make this proclamation resound: God loves you, Christ came for you, Christ is for you 'the Way, the Truth and the Life!' (John 14:6)"[1] This is what serving others is all about.

Of course, Jesus was the consummate servant, for as our memory verse points out, he came "not to be served but to serve." Consequently, the Christian in whom Jesus dwells, who is self-seeking and who is averse to serving others, contradicts the very name he carries; *Christian.* The Holy Trinity was so concerned that we recognize and pursue the opportunity to serve one another that the Father and the Son sent us the indwelling Holy Spirit. He uniquely gifts us with skills beyond our natural talents so that collectively, our abilities and gifts perfectly match the serving opportunities we encounter.

We are to serve everyone, but as Galatians 6:10 and the following quote point out we are to pay special attention to serving our fellow Christians:

> Hence we are to work, and we are to work good and to work it to all so that there is no partiality toward persons. We are to do nothing except do good and good to all. ...However, he [St. Paul] makes the distinction that the good that we work on behalf of all is to be worked most of all on behalf of the household of faith, that is, those who have come to believe and trust in Christ and God.[2]

Questions for Meditation

Mark 10:45 (For context, read Mark 10:35–45)

- In what ways did Jesus serve people?

- What are some specific ways you can follow Jesus' example as a servant?

Galatians 6:10 (For context, read Galatians 5:22–6:10)

- What do you think the writer of Galatians means by verse 5:25?

- How is being an un-serving person a contradiction to living in the Spirit?

- What should determine when we serve others?

- Why do you think this passage underscores the special importance of serving fellow Christians?

Notes

[1] *The Lay Members of Christ's Faithful People*, by Pope John Paul II, 34
[2] Marius Victorinus' commentary on the Epistles to the Galatians, in *Ancient Christian Commentary on Scripture*, Vol. VIII.

Topic: Give Generously

Verses: Proverbs 3:9–10 and 2 Corinthians 9:6–7

▶ Your Plan This Week

1. Complete the topic and reference quiz on pages 87–88.

2. DAILY REVIEW: Series A and C, plus the first ten verses in Series D.

▶ Reflection on the Wisdom of the Church

Isn't it funny how a $10 bill looks so big when you drop it in the church's collection basket, but it looks so small when you try to buy something with it? Our perspective on giving is often affected by the changing value we place on money when we decide to give it away.

> I do not believe one can settle how much we ought to give. I am afraid the only safe rule is to give more than we can spare. In other words, if our expenditure on comforts, luxuries, amusements, etc., is up to the standard common among those with the same income as our own, we are probably giving away too little. If our charities do not at all pinch or hamper us, I should say they are too small.[1]

Jesus spoke a lot about money and treasure. He highly commended those who could only give a little, because the little they gave represented a major portion of what they owned. On the other hand, Jesus questioned the love of those who gave a more significant amount, because it represented such a small portion of what they retained for themselves and were capable of giving. God assigns a value to our giving based on our heart and the spirit in which the gift was given not simply on the size of the gift. Often the amount of money we retain for ourselves is a good indicator of our heart and spirit.

The Church includes generosity as one of the fruits of the Holy Spirit (CCC 1832). Disciples of Jesus Christ should be noted for their generous giving of their time, talent, and treasure—their lives. Disciples of Jesus recognize the resources they have acquired come from a generous and loving God and consequently, they endeavor to care for and use those resources responsibly and generously. They find joy in how much they can share with others, not in how much they can hoard for themselves. In the process of being generous, people discover that Jesus does, in fact, love cheerful and generous givers, and that it is impossible to "out-give" God. Knowing this to be true makes us wonder why we often give so little.

Questions for Meditation

Proverbs 3:9–10 (For context, read Proverbs 3:1–12)

- Proverbs is a collection of wise sayings and moral lessons on life. What are the rewards of putting this wisdom into practice?

- Why do you think the Lord is honored when we give him the first part of our material possessions?

- What is the cause and effect relationship of giving generously?

2 Corinthians 9:6–7 (For context, read 2 Corinthians 9:6–15)

- Why do you think it is important to God that we not give reluctantly or under compulsion?

- What should be involved in helping us "make up our mind" about giving?

- Identify as many benefits of generous giving as you can find in this passage.

Notes

[1] C.S. Lewis in *The Inspirational Writings of C.S. Lewis*, page 332

Fill in the blanks with the correct *topics* and the correct *references* for Series A, B, and C.

A. Live the New Life

B. Proclaim Christ

3. _____
_____
_____

MANKIND   **GOD**

5. _____
_____
_____

1. _____
_____
_____

6. _____
_____
_____

2. _____
_____
_____

7. _____
_____

4. _____
_____
_____

C. Rely on God's Resources

Topic	*Reference*
1. _____	_____ _____
2. _____	_____ _____
3. _____	_____ _____
4. _____	_____ _____
5. _____	_____ _____
6. _____	_____ _____
7. _____	_____ _____

Topic: Develop World Vision

Verses: Acts 1:8 and Matthew 28:19–20

Your Plan This Week

1. Review the "Topic and Reference Quiz" on pages 87–88.

2. DAILY REVIEW: Series A and C, plus the first 12 verses in Series D.

Reflection on the Wisdom of the Church

"It is necessary, then, to keep a watchful eye on this our world, with its problems and values, its unrest and hopes, its defeats and triumphs: … *this* is the field in which the faithful are called to fulfill their mission. Jesus wants them, as he wants all his disciples, to be the 'salt of the earth' and the 'light of the world' (cf. Mt. 5:13–14)."[1]

When God created the world with all of its abundance and created humankind to enjoy and dwell in it, he intended that the greatest joy of life would be for *all* of humanity to enjoy a relationship with him. When Adam and Eve spurned that relationship in pursuit of independence, God put in motion a plan to win them back to abundant life with him. Though he specifically chose to pour out his blessings on a man (Abraham) and a people (Israelites), he always had the salvation of the world in mind.

I will give you as a light to the nations, that my salvation may reach to the end of the earth.[2]

After this I will return, and I will rebuild the dwelling of David, which has fallen; I will rebuild its ruins, and I will set it up, that the rest of men may seek the Lord, and all the Gentiles who are called by my name.[3]

God has the world on his heart, and we who have God on our hearts must also have his love for the salvation of the world on our hearts.

Since Vatican II, the Church has sounded forth the resounding message that her primary task and essential mission is that of evangelization. In addition, our various leaders, especially the last three popes, have consistently included the laity in the task of evangelization. In the words of Pope Paul VI, "it is unthinkable that a person should accept the Word and give himself to the kingdom without becoming a person who bears witness to it and proclaims it in his turn."[4] Jesus' message to today's disciples is still "**Go therefore and make disciples of all nations…**"

Questions for Meditation

Acts 1:8 (For context, read Acts 1:1–11)

- What two promises does Jesus make in this verse?

- What is the significance of "Jerusalem and in all Judea and Samaria and to the ends of the earth"?

- What do you think the disciples thought when Jesus included Samaria in the commission?

- What is your Jerusalem, Judea, and Samaria?

- How do you feel about the responsibility to be a witness to others for Christ?

Matthew 28:19–20 (For context, read Matthew 28:16–20)

- How do you understand Jesus' authority in your life?

- How do laypeople participate in this command?

- What part should this command have in your life's purpose?

- What is the promise of this commission?

Notes

---

[1] *The Lay Members of Christ's Faithful People*, by Pope John Paul II, 3
[2] Isaiah 49:6
[3] Acts 15:16–174
[4] *On Evangelization in the Modern World*, by Pope Paul VI, 24

Grow in Christlikeness

The Christlike life is the only life that can bring glory to God and real meaning to our existence. When our lives take on the character and qualities of Jesus, they become a breath of fresh air to those around us, enabling them to experience the aroma of Jesus Christ through us.

Christlikeness should be the goal for every Christian even though we constantly struggle to not be *conformed* to this world. Many of the passages we have previously memorized and meditated on provide the keys to this transformation into Christ's image. As we meditate on sacred Scripture and allow it to permeate our minds, it remains there to influence our reactions and decisions—and to form Christ's character in us. Sacred Scripture puts it this way, "Have this mind among yourselves, which is yours in Christ Jesus (Philippians 2:5). **Christlikeness is not something we can just tack on to our lives; it must spring from his life within us.**

> *He belongs to you, but more than that, he longs to be in you, living and ruling in you, as the head lives and rules in the body. He desires that whatever is in him may live and rule in you: his breath in your breath, his heart in your heart, all the faculties of his soul in the faculties of your soul, so that these words may be fulfilled in you: Glorify God and bear him in your body, that the life of Jesus may be made manifest in you.*[1]

The verses you will be memorizing in the next seven weeks focus on various attitudinal characteristics of Jesus. These characteristics affect how we relate to people and how we behave toward them and toward situations we encounter in life, especially the more difficult ones. When people observe us responding to difficult people and difficult situations in a godly manner, they recognize and know what Jesus is like, and they find hope.

Series E: Grow in Christlikeness presents 14 passages to help you focus attention on the character of Christ:

Love—John 13:34–35 and 1 John 3:18
Humility—Philippians 2:3–4 and 1 Peter 5:5–6
Purity—Ephesians 5:3–4 and 1 Peter 2:11
Honesty—Ephesians 4:25 and Acts 24:16
Faith—Hebrews 11:6 and Romans 4:20–21
Good Works—Ephesians 2:10 and Matthew 5:16
Do God's Will—Ephesians 5:17 and 1 Peter 4:1–2

[1] From a treatise on the admirable heart of Jesus by Saint Eudes, LOH, Vol, IV, page 1331

Topic: Love

Verses: John 13:34–35 and 1 John 3:18

▶ **Your Plan This Week**

DAILY REVIEW: Series A and D.

▶ **Reflection on the Wisdom of the Church**

As 1 John 4:10 points out, "This is love, not that we loved God but that he loved us and sent his Son to be the expiation for our sins." God's love for us is shown through Jesus' incarnation and passion and defines what true love really is. *Agape* is the Greek term used to define this type of love, a love which is self-sacrificing in nature. However, most of us use the word "love" to refer to our emotional response to others in whom we have self-interest, such as a member of our family, a person with whom we have a romantic connection, or someone with whom we share a similar passion or interest. Consequently, we need the Holy Spirit to help us truly understand and redefine what Christ-like love is all about.

The *Catechism* makes clear that self-sacrificing love is best directed toward those from whom we have nothing to gain: "Christ died out of love for us, while we were still 'enemies.' The Lord asks us to love as he does, even our *enemies*, to make ourselves the neighbor of those farthest away, and to love children and the poor as Christ himself."[1] Loving *sacrificially* is being like Christ and is the strongest evidence that Christ lives in us.

Saint Thomas á Kempis reminds us that love is the "more excellent way" of which Saint Paul speaks in 1 Corinthians 13.

> *Without love, the outward work is of no value; but whatever is done out of love, be it ever so little, is wholly fruitful. For God regards the greatness of the love that prompts a man, rather than the greatness of his achievement.*[2]

Love is the mark of a disciple who follows and desires to be like Christ. It is more than a feeling or a sentimental reaction. Love "prompts a man" (or woman) to action and to sacrifice. This prompting to *action love* should normally be reflected in how Christ's followers love others.

Questions for Meditation

John 13:34–35 (For context, read John 13:31–38)

- Whose example of love are we to follow?
- How would you describe the way Jesus loves?
- What results can we expect when we practice this kind of love?

1 John 3:18 (For context, read 1 John 3:15–24)

- According to this passage, what are some ways we express love?
- Which is easiest or most difficult for you?
- How does this passage illustrate that love for God is expressed by action love for others?

Notes

---

[1] *Catechism of the Catholic Church* 1825
[2] Thomas à Kempis, *The Imitation of Christ*, page 43

Topic: Humility

Verses: Philippians 2:3–4 and 1 Peter 5:5–6

▶ Your Plan This Week

DAILY REVIEW: Series B and D, plus the first two verses in Series E.

▶ Reflections on the Wisdom of the Church

For the Christian, God has provided several means of grace which enable a person to experience God's blessings more completely. Humility is one of those means of grace, as our second memory verse points out:, "He gives grace to the humble." What a marvelous promise and source of motivation!

Humility is not a virtue in the eyes of the world, but it truly has been elevated to a virtue by the life of Jesus, who describes himself as meek and lowly of heart. Humility is not so much thinking poorly of oneself as it is choosing not to think about yourself as the most important concern in your life. Rather, as Jesus showed us, humility is considering others as vitally important and serving them as though they were more important than one's own self, perhaps even to the point of sacrificing for them. "It does you no harm when you esteem all others better than yourself, but it does you great harm when you esteem yourself above others."[1]

We are able to grow in humility as we look at the life of Christ who, though God in the flesh, did not grasp after and demand his rights as one equal to God. The circumstances surrounding Jesus' Incarnation reflect his humility and willingness to lay aside his divine rights.

> *What wondrous humility, what marvelous poverty! The King of angels, the Lord of heaven and earth resting in a manger! Look more deeply into the mirror and meditate on his humility,... ponder his unspeakable love which caused him to suffer on the wood of the cross and to endure the most shameful kind of death.* [2]

It is not self-abasement that brings about humility; rather, it is a deep meditation upon the humility of Jesus. As we meditate on Jesus' profound self-giving through his Incarnation, life, and Passion, the humble aspect of his character will be reflected back in our lives as the virtue of humility.

Questions for Meditation

Philippians 2:3–4 (For context, read Philippians 2:1–11)

- What motivation for pursuing humility is included in this passage?
- What does this passage imply about a spirit of self-interest and self-promotion?
- What motives for action are we to avoid completely?
- What or who is the source of humility and how does one attain it?

1 Peter 5:5–6 (For context, read 1 Peter 5:1–11)

- Is humility more a matter of action or a matter of attitude? Why?
- How does a person humble themself?
- What are the chief benefits of behaving with humility?

Notes

---

[1] Thomas à Kempis, *The Imitation of Christ*, Book 1, Chapter 7
[2] From a letter by Saint Clare, LOH, Vol. IV, page 1311

Topic: Purity

Verses: Ephesians 5:3–4 and 1 Peter 2:11

Your Plan This Week

1. Take the self-checking quiz on pages 99–101.
2. DAILY REVIEW: Series C and D, plus the first four verses in Series E.

Reflection on the Wisdom of the Church

Perhaps the most counter-cultural behavior we can exhibit in Western society is a commitment to pure thoughts, words, and deeds. Over the last 40 years, our society has become amazingly crude in its use of language and blatantly erotic and sensual in its arts and media. Pornography is rampant, and children are being exposed to sex and sexuality at an increasingly early age. This should not be so. Yet, conformity to and tolerance of, this cultural deterioration is often no different for many Christians than it is for non-Christians.

God is holy and calls us to holy living. Impurity wars against our souls and undermines our witness, whereas the development of a pure life empowers us and attracts the non-Christian to Christ. "It often happens that pagans who once reviled the faith of Christians, because they had abandoned their gods, stop doing so after they see what a holy and pure life they lead in Christ. They begin instead to glorify and praise God, who is shown by acts of goodness and righteousness to be good and righteous himself."[1]

The focus or call to purity is not a diabolical scheme to prevent us from enjoying one of the most precious gifts of God, our human sexuality. Rather, God designed it to set us free thus enabling us to enjoy it to its fullness.

Chastity [sexual purity] includes an apprenticeship in self-mastery which is a training in human freedom. The alternative is clear: either man governs his passions and finds peace, or he lets himself be dominated by them and becomes unhappy. Man's dignity therefore requires him to act out of conscious and free choice, as moved and drawn in a personal way from within, and not by blind impulses in himself or by mere external constraint. Man gains such dignity when, ridding himself of all slavery to the passions, he presses forward to his goal by freely choosing what is good...[2]

Sacred Scripture warns us in Proverbs 25:28 that "A man without self-control is like a city broken into and left without walls"—defenseless.

Questions for Meditation

Ephesians 5:3–4 (For context, read Ephesians 5:1–14)

- What behaviors are forbidden in these verses?
- What is there about the nature of these three behaviors that make them wrong and unlike God?
- Ultimately, what is the purpose for living an exemplary life?

1 Peter 2:11 (For context, read 1 Peter 2:1–12)

- How does Saint Peter describe us (vs 1–10)?
- Why should impure language and actions be avoided?
- What is the significance of Saint Peter's reference to us as "strangers and aliens"?
- What affect does yielding to sinful desires have on us?
- What is one of the chief benefits of behaving with purity?

Notes

[1] *On 1 Peter*, by Bede, from *Ancient Christian Commentary on Scripture*, Vol. XI, page 91
[2] *Catechism of the Catholic Church* 2339

1. Two essentials for a successful Scripture memory program are … (Check the *two* best answers.)
   ☐ a. jotting down references of verses you want to learn later.
   ☐ b. marking memorized verses in your Bible.
   ☐ c. consistently memorizing new verses each week.
   ☐ d. following a regular, daily program of reviewing verses you have learned.

2. If memorizing new verses ever becomes routine or lifeless, these things could be done: (Check the *two* best answers.)
   ☐ a. Stop memorizing for a month or six weeks.
   ☐ b. Spend more time praying over and meditating on your verses.
   ☐ c. Find a new way of memorizing.
   ☐ d. Begin using the verses more in conversation and in letters.

3. Indicate with letters (A–E) the proper order of the five series of verses in the *Catholic Topical Memory System*.
   _____ Rely on God's Resources
   _____ Grow in Christlikeness
   _____ Proclaim Christ
   _____ Live the New Life
   _____ Be Christ's Disciple

4. Add the missing information in this outline of the first four series in the *Catholic Topical Memory System:*

   A. Live the New Life
      1. Christ the Center

      _____
      Galatians 2:20
      2. Sacramental Life

      _____
      Acts 2:41a–42
      3. Obedience to Christ
         Romans 12:2

      _____
      4. _____
         2 Timothy 3:16

      _____

5. Prayer

_____
Philippians 4:6–7
6. Community

_____

_____

7. Evangelization
Matthew 4:19

_____

B. Proclaim Christ
1. _____
Romans 3:23
2. _____

_____
Hebrews 9:27
3. Christ Paid the Penalty

_____
1 Peter 3:18
4. _____
Ephesians 2:8,9
Titus 3:5
5. Personal Response

_____
Romans 10:9–10
6. _____

_____
1 John 5:13
7. Be Baptized

_____

_____

C. Rely on God's Resources
1. His Spirit

_____

_____

2. His Presence

_____

_____

3. His Strength
Isaiah 41:10

_____

4. _____

   Numbers 23:19

5. His Peace
   Isaiah 26:3

   _____

6. His Provision
   Romans 8:32

   _____

7. _____

   Hebrews 2:18

   _____

D. Be Christ's Disciple

1. Put Christ First

   _____

   Luke 9:23

2. _____

   _____

   Romans 12:1

3. Confess Sin

   _____

   1 John 1:9

4. Be Steadfast
   1 Corinthians 15:58

   _____

5. Serve Others

   _____

   _____

6. _____

   _____

   2 Corinthians 9:6–7

7. _____

   Acts 1:8

   _____

Correct Answers:
1. C and D
2. B and D
3. C, E, B, A, and D
4. See the Checklist on page XX

Topic: Honesty

Verses: Ephesians 4:25 and Acts 24:16

▶ **Your Plan This Week**

DAILY REVIEW: Series A and D, plus the first six verses in Series E.

▶ **Reflection on the Wisdom of the Church**

It is written, The mouth that lies destroys the soul. ... Therefore the apostle puts truth telling in the first place when he commands us to put off the old nature, under which name all sins are understood, saying therefore, putting off lying speak the truth.[1]

Inasmuch as we have been created in truth and righteousness we should live a life free from dishonesty. However, for many Christians honesty, like truth, is relative, based on a malformed conscience. Consequently, understanding the guilt or innocence of our behavior depends on the condition of our conscience, which Scripture indicates can being either good, weak, seared, evil/guilty, cleansed, or clear. Thus it is vitally important to maintain our conscience by being honest and practicing integrity in all we do or say. A willingness to entertain dishonesty in our lives not only creates guilt, but also recreates our conscience into something less than what God desires.

Guilt is directly connected to the spiritual condition of our conscience. Our conscience is a witness to ourselves as to whether some action or attitude is wrong. With a little research, we find that the New Testament writers referred to a variety of different spiritual conditions under which our conscience can operate.[2]

A person ruled by a good conscience, which has been formed by the Holy Spirit, reflects the nature of the Father and the character of the Son. Jesus referred to himself in John 14:6 as the way, the truth, and the life. Jesus is the truth. By knowing him we know what is true about God and humanity, and what is true about life and eternity. Being followers of the truth and practicing truthfulness in all our relationships will enable us to be like a light shining in a dark place. Honesty will attract others to Christ, the source of integrity within us.

Questions for Meditation

Ephesians 4:25 (For context, read Ephesians 4:17–31)

- What forms of dishonesty are forbidden in these verses?
- Which one of these three is most difficult for you to control?
- Why do you think being honest in all areas of life is so important to God?

Acts 24:16 (For context, read Acts 24:10–21)

- How important is our conscience?
- Is it possible to have a clear conscience toward man, but not toward God, or vice versa?
- What caused Paul to maintain a blameless conscience?
- How does this passage illustrate the empowerment that a life of integrity brings?

Notes

[1] Saint Augustine, "On Lying," in *Ancient Christian Commentary on Scripture,* Vol. VIII
[2] *The Seven Last Words of Christ,* by Rich Cleveland, page 14

Topic: Faith

Verses: Hebrews 11:6 and Romans 4:20–21

▶ **Your Plan This Week**

DAILY REVIEW: Series B and D, plus the first eight verses in Series E.

▶ **Reflection on the Wisdom of the Church**

Jesus often spoke about the importance of having faith. He refers to some as "Ye of little faith." He commends others, in some cases non-Israelites, for their "great faith." He frequently chides his followers with the question, "Where is your faith?" His disciples, in turn, implored him, "increase our faith."

Where does this faith come from; how is it expressed?

Faith is an entirely free gift that God makes to man. We can lose this priceless gift, as St. Paul indicated to St. Timothy: "Wage the good warfare, holding faith and a good conscience. By rejecting conscience, certain persons have made shipwreck of their faith." To live, grow, and persevere in the faith until the end we must nourish it with the word of God; we must beg the Lord to increase our faith; it must be "working through charity," abounding in hope, and rooted in the faith of the Church.[1]

By faith, man completely submits his intellect and his will to God. With his whole being man gives his assent to God the revealer. Sacred Scripture calls this human response to God, the author of revelation, "obedience of faith."[2]

This "obedience of faith" is what introduces us to life in Christ as we respond to his invitation to receive new life in God. Such obedience should be one of the chief characteristics of experiencing that life. It involves a cognizant acceptance of, and a willingness to act upon, facts about God.

Faith involves believing God with our whole being. When all is going well, faith is easy and we can almost function without an awareness of its presence. However, it is faith that carries us though adversity. We are like Christ when we trust in the Father's will. Saint Theresa assures us of this point in the following poem:

Let nothing trouble you / Let nothing frighten you / Everything passes / God never changes / Patience / Obtains all / Whoever has God / Wants for nothing / God alone is enough.[3]

Questions for Meditation

Hebrews 11:6 (For context, read Hebrews 11:1–16)

- In this passage, which example of faith is most significant to you? Why?

- How does Hebrews 11:1 define faith?

- What is the difference between believing that God exists and believing that God rewards those who seek him?

- What is involved in "diligently seeking God"?

Romans 4:20–21 (For context, read Romans 4:16–21)

- According to this passage what elements enabled Abraham to grow in faith?

- Give some examples of God's promises on which we can rely and which should influence our lives today?

- How is lack of faith manifested?

Notes

---

[1] *Catechism of the Catholic Church* 162
[2] Ibid., 143
[3] Ibid., 227

Topic: Good Works

Verses: Ephesians 2:10 and Matthew 5:16

Your Plan This Week

1. DAILY REVIEW: Series C and D, plus the first ten verses in Series E.

2. Read "How to Keep Learning and Reviewing" on page 114.

Reflection on the Wisdom of the Church

The debate over the role of faith and works in our salvation has been one of the most divisive arguments in the life of Christendom. It has caused some to diminish the importance of one aspect to the exclusion of the other. Yet, salvation is God's idea, and he is the one who determines the interrelationship between these two. He did not leave us devoid of insight on this; rather, he provided wisdom and clarity through divine revelation.

The Epistle of Saint James is one source of revelation. It accurately ties together the relationship between our life of faith and our life of works. He explains that to have faith without works is like being a hearer only and not a practitioner of faith, and he questions whether that kind of faith is effectual to save a person. He goes on to say it is our works which manifest our faith to others (James 2:18). *It is a life of good works which witnesses to the truth of the Gospel.*

Though Saint Paul writes that works cannot initiate our salvation, he also says God creates new life within us to enable us to spend our life performing the good works he prepared and purposed for each of us to do (Ephesians 2:8–10).

The revelatory wisdom of the Church also affirms the role of good works: "While faith provides the basis for works, the *strength* of faith comes out only in works."[1] In one of his sermons, Pope Leo explains that both Saint James and Saint Paul used the example of Abraham to show this interdependence of faith and works.

> *For the same Abraham is at different times an example of both kinds of faith. The first is prebaptismal faith, which does not require works but only confession and the word of salvation, by which those who believe in Christ are justified. The second is postbaptismal faith, which is combined with works. Understood in this way, the two apostles do not contradict one another, but one and the same Spirit is speaking through both of them.[2]*

It is through this marriage of faith and works—of faith generating good works—that God creates as our salvation and for which we are called his "workmanship."

Questions for Meditation

Ephesians 2:10 (For context, read Ephesians 2:4–10)

- Why do you think God ordained that we should live a life of good works?

- How are you living out this ordination in your life?

- In the context of this passage, is good works a means or an effect of our salvation?

Matthew 5:16 (For context, read Matthew 5:13–20)

- Why do you think good works are analogous to a light?

- What is one of God's purposes in our maintaining a life of good works?

- What is the difference between doing good works as "light" to be seen by others, and doing good works to impress others?

Notes

---

[1] A sermon by Pope Leo the Great, from *Ancient Christian Commentary on Scripture*, Vol. XI, page 29. Emphasis added

[2] The monk Andreas, from *Ancient Christian Commentary on Scripture*, Vol. XI, page 32

Topic: Do God's Will

Verses: Ephesians 5:17 and 1 Peter 4:1–2

Your Plan This Week

1. DAILY REVIEW: Series A and B, plus the first twelve verses in Series E.

2. Complete the "Topic and Reference Quiz" at the end of this lesson on pages 110–113.

Reflection on the Wisdom of the Church

Jesus arrived at Jacob's well tired and hungry. When the disciples returned with food urging him to eat they found Jesus refreshed, through having spent the time ministering the Good News to the Samaritan woman who came to the well. Jesus explained, "I have food to eat of which you do not know ... My food is to do the will of him who sent me, and to accomplish his work." (John 4:34)

This characteristic of understanding and doing the will of the Father was central to Jesus' life and ministry. Consequently, at the end of his earthly life when he is facing betrayal, brutality, and death on the cross we see him praying, "My Father, if it be possible, let this cup pass from me; nevertheless, not as I will, but as thou wilt ... My Father, if this cannot pass unless I drink it, thy will be done."

Early in Jesus' ministry he taught the disciples to think, live and pray "Thy will be done, on earth as it is in heaven." Like an ancient mariner orienting his journey in relationship to the North Star, so Jesus' disciples must learn to orient their lives in relationship to the Father's will. This is a true indication that we are members of God's family, "For whoever does the will of my Father in heaven is my brother, and sister, and mother." (John 12:50)

> Many people think they know what God's will is, and they are mistaken. Those who do not have a renewed mind err and go wrong. It is not every mind but only one which is renewed and conformed (as I say) to the image of God which can tell whether what we think, say and do in particular instances is the will of God or not.
>
> ... Because the will of God is something good and acceptable and perfect, there is no doubt that it is pleasing to God. For God cannot will anything which is not good, and if something is good and perfect, then it must be pleasing to God.[1]

Doing God's will is a Christlike characteristic of promise, for we are told that the person who does God's will "abides for ever." (1 John 2:17)

Questions for Meditation

Ephesians 5:17 (For context, read Ephesians 5:6–20)

- This passage talks about being deceived (vs. 6) and being foolish (vs.17). What are some evidences of a deceived or foolish believer?

- What have you found helpful in discerning "what is pleasing to the Lord" (vs. 10) and "what the will of the Lord is" (vs. 17)?

- What are some evidences of a wise believer whose life is oriented around doing the Father's will?

1 Peter 4:1–2 (For context, read 1 Peter 4:1–11)

- How does this passage define living according to the will of God?

- How do your personal desires interface with doing God's will?

- How do you feel about this attribute of Christlikeness?

Notes

---

[1] Commentary on the Epistle to the Romans, by Origen, from Ancient Christian Commentary on Scripture, Vol. VI, page 308.

Use the blank spaces to fill in the series names, the topics, and the reference for the complete *Topical Memory System.*

A. _____

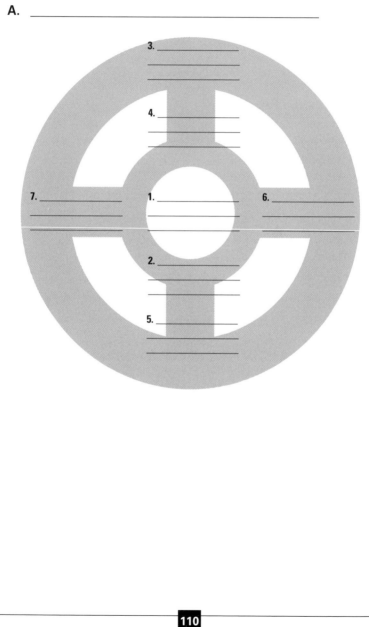

B. _____

        3. _____
          _____
          _____

MANKIND   **GOD**

                               5. _____
                                  _____

1. _____
   _____
   _____   6. _____
                                  _____

2. _____
   _____
   _____   7. _____
                                  _____

         4. _____
           _____
           _____

C. _____

Topic   *Reference*

1. _____   _____
                           _____

2. _____   _____
                           _____

3. _____   _____
                           _____

4. _____   _____
                           _____

5. _____   _____
                           _____

6. _____   _____
                           _____

7. _____   _____
                           _____

D. _____

Topic	Reference
1. _____	_____
	_____
2. _____	_____
	_____
3. _____	_____
	_____
4. _____	_____
	_____
5. _____	_____
	_____
6. _____	_____
	_____
7. _____	_____
	_____

E. _____

Topic   Reference

1. _____   _____

                                _____

2. _____   _____

                                _____

3. _____   _____

                                _____

4. _____   _____

                                _____

5. _____   _____

                                _____

6. _____   _____

                                _____

7. _____   _____

                                _____

How to Keep Reviewing and Learning

Keep reviewing

Someone has wisely said that we often forget what we should remember and remember what we should forget. Forgetting comes naturally to us, so you must expend effort reviewing the verses you have learned in order to retain them. A simple, workable review system will help you.

For the first few weeks after memorizing Series E, you will especially want to concentrate on reviewing those 14 verses. Here's a simple plan you can follow:

WEEK 1— Daily review: Series A, B, and E.
WEEK 2— Daily review: Series C, D, and E.
WEEK 3— Daily review: Series A, B, and E.
WEEK 4— Daily review: Series C, D, and E.

After the fourth week, you may want to review one of the five series each day of the week. For example, review Series A on Monday, Series B on Tuesday, and so on through the week.

**Don't lose what you have worked so hard to obtain!
Be faithful in reviewing your verses!**

Use the "buddy system"

Self-discipline is hard, so try to find someone to help you regularly review your memorized verses. This "buddy" could be your spouse, one of your children, a friend, or a co-worker.

What about learning new verses?

You may already have a list of verses for future memory—verses that have impressed you from your daily Scripture reading, from a homily, or from a conversation with a friend who shared the verses with you. You will want to continue memorizing and meditating on key Scripture portions so the Holy Spirit can draw them from your memory to use in your life and ministry.

Set a goal now of learning and meditating on one, two, or three new verses each week. You can place these under the same topics you learned in the *Catholic Topical Memory System,* or you can give them new topic titles of your own choosing.

Be sure to continually revise your review system to include regular review of the new verses you are learning.

Expanding your review system

As you learn more verses, it will naturally take more time and effort to review and keep them all sharp in your memory. Having a systematic review plan will become increasingly important.

One of the simplest foundations for a good review system is to arrange all your verses according to the books of the Bible and arranging all the verses *within each book* according to chapter and verse.

Congratulations!

You are to be commended for expending a great deal of time and effort to fill your heart and mind with holy Scripture. Completing this course has undoubtedly been a significant, life-changing accomplishment for you. We pray that God will bless and reward you for your effort and devotion to him and his written word; may it increasingly become a source of nourishment and strength.

We would love to hear from you about how scripture memory has impacted your life. Please write or email us at:

Emmaus Journey
PO Box 63587
Colorado Springs, CO 80962-3587

Email: info@emmausjourney.org

Acknowledgements

1. à Kempis, Thomas. The Imitation of Christ.
2. Ancient Christian Commentary on Scripture, Volumes IX and XI.
3. Brown, Raymond. The Anchor Bible, Vol. 29A.
4. "Catechesis in Our Time." Pope John Paul II.
5. Catechism of the Catholic Church.
6. Catholic encyclopedia.
7. Cleveland, Rich. Living in the Power of the Holy Spirit.
8. Ibid. The Seven Last Words of Christ.
9. General Directory of Catechesis. The Vatican.
10. Hall, Christopher A. Reading Scripture with the Church Fathers
11. Jean-Marie Cardinal Lustiger. Dare to Believe.
12. Lewis, C.S. The Inspirational Writings of C.S. Lewis.
13. Liturgy of the Hours. Volumes II, III and IV.
14. McBrien, Richard P. Catholicism.
15. Pope John Paul II. Mission of the Redeemer.
16. Nouwen, Fr. Henri J. Can You Drink This Cup.
17. Pope John Paul II. On the Eucharist in Its Relationship to the Church.
18. Pope Paul VI. On Evangelization in the Modern World.
19. Pastoral Constitution in the Modern World.
20. Pope John XXIII. I Will Be Called John.
21. Ibid. Journal of a Soul.
22. Pope John Paul II. Mission of the Redeemer.
23. Pope John Paul I. Illustrissimi: Letters from Pope John Paul I.
24. Saint Catherine of Siena. The Dialogue. Translation by Suzanne Noffke, O.P. Paulist Press.
25. Saint Elizabeth Ann Seton. The Soul of Elizabeth Ann Seton.
26. Saint Francis de Sales. Introduction to the Devout Life.
27. Ibid. The Art of Loving God.
28. Ibid. The Art of Loving God. (Conference V).
29. Saint John Chrysostom. De Anna.
30. "Stewardship: A Disciple's Response." National Council of Catholic Bishops.
31. "The Dogmatic Constitution on Divine Revelation." VI, 21 by Vatican II.
32. Pope John Paul II. The Lay Members of Christ's Faithful People.
33. Von Hildebrand, Dietrich. Transformation in Christ.

Emmaus Journey
Catholic Small-Group Resources

The vision of *Emmaus Journey* is to help Catholics mature in Christ, to grow in their understanding and commitment to sacred Scripture and Church teachings, and to fan into flame people's commitment to prayer and evangelization.

Emmaus Journey contributes to this goal by helping parish leaders inaugurate small-groups and small Christian communities within their parishes; assisting in the training of small-group facilitators; and providing practical small-group resources.

Emmaus Journey small-group materials integrate Scripture study with meaningful support materials from Church teachings and Catholic leaders, using a practical topical approach. These studies provide an effective addition to existing adult formation resources and are available at a reasonable cost.

In addition *Emmaus Journey* provides effective formation materials and training resources in various multi-media formats. Decades of ministry experience in evangelization and disciple-making are reflected in these practical training tools. These resources will impact your life and enhance your ministry, and can be found on the Emmaus Journey web page.

Please visit www.emmausjourney.org for our latest materials.

Personal Response

John 1:12   RSVCE

But to all who received him, who believed in his name, he gave power to become children of God.

Jo n 1:12

B-9 Proclaim Christ

Unmerited Salvation

Ephesians 2:8–9   RSVCE

For by grace you have been saved tɦrouɡh faith; and this is not your own doing, it iʂ the gift of God not because of works, leʂt anˀ man should boast.

Ephesian 2:8-9

B-7 Proclaim Christ

Christ Paid the Penalty

Romans 5:8   RSVCE

But God shows his love for us in that whịle we were yet sinners Christ died for us.

Romaɴs 5:8

B-5 Proclaim Christ

His Spirit

John 14:26   RSVCE

"But the Counselor, the Holy Spirit, whom the Father will send in my name, he will teach you all things, and bring to your remembrance all that I have said to you."

John 14:26

C-1 Rely on God's Resources

Be Baptized

Acts 2:38   RSVCE

And Peter said to them, "Repent, and be baptized every one of you in the name of Jesus Christ for the forgiveness of your sins; and you shall receive the gift of the Holy Spirit.

Acts 2:38

B-13 Proclaim Christ

Assurance of God's Mercy

Philippians 1:6   RSVCE

And I am sure that he who began a good work in you will bring it to completion at the day of Jesus Christ.

Philippians 1:6

B-11 Proclaim Christ

His Faithfulness

Lamentations 3:22–23   RSVCE

The steadfast love of the LORD never ceases, his mercies never come to an end; they are new every morning; great is thy faithfulness.

Lamentations 3:22–23

C-7 Rely on God's Resources

His Strength

Isaiah 41:10   RSVCE

"Fear not, for I am with you, be not dismayed, for I am your God; I will strengthen you, I will help you, I will uphold you with my victorious right hand."

Isaiah 41:10

C-5 Rely on God's Resources

His Presence

1 Corinthians 10:16   RSVCE

The cup of blessing which we bless, is it not a participation in the blood of Christ? The bread which we break, is it not a participation in the body of Christ?

1 Corinthians 10:16

C-3 Rely on God's Resources

Christated the Penalty · Christ Paid the Penalty
1 Peter 3:18 — RSVCE

For Christ also died for sins once for all, the righteous for the unrighteous, that he might bring us to God, being put to death in the flesh but made alive in the spirit.

1 Peter 3:18

B-6 Proclaim Christ

Unmerited Salvation
Titus 3:5 — RSVCE

He saved us, not because of deeds done by us in righteousness, but in virtue of his own mercy, by the washing of regeneration and renewal in the Holy Spirit.

Titus 3:5

B-8 Proclaim Christ

Personal Response
Romans 10:9-10 — RSVCE

Because, if you confess with your lips that Jesus is Lord and believe in your heart that God raised him from the dead, you will be saved. For man believes with his heart and so is justified, and he confesses with his lips and so is saved.

Romans 10:9-10

B-10 Proclaim Christ

Assurance of God's Mercy
1 John 5:13 — RSVCE

I write this to you who believe in the name of the Son of God, that you may know that you have eternal life.

1 John 5:13

B-12 Proclaim Christ

Be Baptized
Galatians 3:26-27 — RSVCE

For in Christ Jesus you are all sons of God, through faith. For as many of you as were baptized into Christ have put on Christ.

Galatians 3:26-27

B-14 Proclaim Christ

His Presence
John 6:55-56 — RSVCE

"For my flesh is food indeed, and my blood is drink indeed. He who eats my flesh and drinks my blood abides in me, and I in him."

John 6:55-56

C-4 Rely on God's Resources

His Strength
Philippians 4:13 — RSVCE

I can do all things in him who strengthens me.

Philippians 4:13

C-6 Rely on God's Resources

His Spirit
1 Corinthians 2:12 — RSVCE

Now we have received not the spirit of the world, but the Spirit which is from God, that we might understand the gifts bestowed on us by God.

1 Corinthians 2:12

C-8 Rely on God's Resources

His Faithfulness
Numbers 23:19 — RSVCE

God is not man, that he should lie, or a son of man, that he should repent. Has he said, and will he not do it? Or has he spoken, and will he not fulfill it?

Numbers 23:19

C-2 Rely on God's Resources

His Help In Temptation

Hebrews 2:18   RSVCE

For because he himself has suffered and been tempted, he is able to help those who are tempted.

Hebrews 2:18

C-13 Rely on God's Resources

His Provision

Ephesians 6:10–11   RSVCE

Finally, be strong in the Lord and in the strength of his might. Put on the whole armor of God, that you may be able to stand against the wiles of the devil.

Ephesians 6:10–11

C-11 Rely on God's Resources

His Peace

Isaiah 26:3   RSVCE

Thou dost keep him in perfect peace, whose mind is stayed on thee, because he trusts in thee.

Isaiah 26:3

C-9 Rely on God's Resources

Confess Sin

Psalm 32:5   RSVCE

I acknowledged my sin to thee, and I did not hide my iniquity; I said, "I will confess my transgressions to the LORD"; then thou didst forgive the guilt of my sin.

Psalm 32:5

D-5 Be Christ's Disciple

Pursue Holiness

1 John 2:15–16   RSVCE

Do not love the world or the things in the world. If any one loves the world, love for the Father is not in him. For all that is in the world, the lust of the flesh and the lust of the eyes and the pride of life, is not of the Father but is of the world.

1 John 2:15–16

D-3 Be Christ's Disciple

Put Christ First

Matthew 6:33   RSVCE

"But seek first his kingdom and his righteousness, and all these things shall be yours as well."

Matthew 6:33

D-1 Be Christ's Disciple

Give Generously

Proverbs 3:9–10   RSVCE

Honor the LORD with your substance and with the first fruits of all your produce; then your barns will be filled with plenty, and your vats will be bursting with wine.

Proverbs 3:9–10

D-11 Be Christ's Disciple

Serve Others

Mark 10:45   RSVCE

"For the Son of man also came not to be served but to serve, and to give his life as a ransom for many."

Mark 10:45

D-9 Be Christ's Disciple

Be Steadfast

1 Corinthians 15:58   RSVCE

Therefore, my beloved brethren, be steadfast, immovable, always abounding in the work of the Lord, knowing that in the Lord your labor is not in vain.

1 Corinthians 15:58

D-7 Be Christ's Disciple

His Peace

1 Peter 5:7 — RSVCE

Cast all your anxieties on him, for he cares about you.

1 Peter 5:7

C-10 Rely on God's Resources

His Provision

Philippians 4:19 — RSVCE

And my God will supply every need of yours according to his riches in glory in Christ Jesus.

Philippians 4:19

C-12 Rely on God's Resources

His Help In Temptation

1 Corinthians 10:13 — RSVCE

No temptation has overtaken you that is not common to man. God is faithful, and he will not let you be tempted beyond your strength, but with the temptation will also provide the way of escape, that you may be able to endure it.

1 Corinthians 10:13

C-14 Rely on God's Resources

Put Christ First

Luke 9:23 — RSVCE

And he said to all, "If any man would come after me, let him deny himself and take up his cross daily and follow me."

Luke 9:23

D-2 Be Christ's Disciple

Pursue Holiness

Romans 12:1 — RSVCE

I appeal to you therefore, brethren, by the mercies of God, to present your bodies as a living sacrifice, holy and acceptable to God, which is your spiritual worship.

Romans 12:1

D-4 Be Christ's Disciple

Confess Sin

1 John 1:9 — RSVCE

If we confess our sins, he is faithful and just, and will forgive our sins and cleanse us from all unrighteousness.

1 John 1:9

D-6 Be Christ's Disciple

Be Steadfast

Hebrews 12:3 — RSVCE

Consider him who endured from sinners such hostility against himself, so that you may not grow weary or fainthearted.

Hebrews 12:3

D-8 Be Christ's Disciple

Serve Others

Galatians 6:10 — RSVCE

So then, as we have opportunity, let us do good to all men, and especially to those who are of the household of faith.

Galatians 6:10

D-10 Be Christ's Disciple

Give Generously

2 Corinthians 9:6-7 — RSVCE

The point is this: he who sows sparingly will also reap sparingly, and he who sows bountifully will also reap bountifully. Each one must do as he has made up his mind, not reluctantly or under compulsion, for God loves a cheerful giver.

2 Corinthians 9:6-7

D-12 Be Christ's Disciple